NORF GHOSTS & LEGENDS

SCANDALS, SIEGES & SPOOKS

PAMELA BROOKS

best wishes

Pamela Brooks

HALSGROVE

First published in Great Britain in 2008

Copyright Pamela Brooks © 2008

British Library Cataloguing-in-Publication Data
A CIP record for this title is available from the British Library

All images by Pamela Brooks, except pages 53 and 93, courtesy of Norfolk County Council Library and Information Service

Cover image shows Baconsthorpe Castle

ISBN 978 1 84114 747 5

HALSGROVE
Halsgrove House
Ryelands Industrial Estate, Bagley Road,
Wellington, Somerset TA21 9PZ
Tel: 01823 653777
Fax: 01823 216796
email: sales@halsgrove.com
website: www.halsgrove.com

Printed and bound by Short Run Press Ltd., Exeter

Contents

For Gerard,
Christopher and Chloë,
with all my love

Preface

Ever since I was a tiny child (small enough to be scared by the polar bear in Norwich castle!) I've been fascinated by the castles and the monastic ruins in Norfolk. We have some incredibly beautiful ruins in our county, and there are fascinating human stories behind the stones. Stories of sieges and bloodshed, of visionaries and ghosts, and of scandals among the monks and nuns.

Although there are many more castles and priories in the county than I've included here, not all have legends or tales attached; I've focused on the ones with the most interesting stories. I hope you enjoy reading these as much as I've enjoyed researching them.

This is also the place where I would like to say thank you. First of all to my husband Gerard and my children Christopher and Chloë, for their enthusiasm in going exploring and visiting all the sites covered in this book (and especially to Gerard for putting up with my habit of directing him down very narrow lanes, to find a tiny bit of masonry in a distant field). To Dot Lumley, my agent, as always for her support, encouragement and wisdom. To Simon Butler at Halsgrove, for giving me the chance to tell these stories. And, last but not least, very grateful thanks to Norfolk County Library and Information Services (particularly to Clare Agate, Janice Rix and the staff at the Heritage Centre and Helen at Costessey Library) for help with finding texts and the loan of photographs.

Pamela Brooks, 2008

Baconsthorpe Castle

Baconsthorpe Castle.

Baconsthorpe Castle is the remains of a late medieval and Tudor fortified and moated manor house. It lies just north of the village of Baconsthorpe, about three miles east of Holt (OS map reference TG 121 381).

Beginnings of the house

The house was started in 1450 by the lawyer Sir John Heydon, who was born the son of William Baxter, a peasant in Heydon. John changed his surname from his family name to the name of his village, probably to diguise his humble beginnings. He was appointed as the recorder of Norwich in 1431, though he was dismissed in 1437 because he was unpopular and was accused of giving the city's documents to Norwich Cathedral priory during a dispute. The row came to a head in Gladman's Insurrection (see Norwich Cathedral Priory, page 107).

By 1450 Heydon was a justice of the peace and had a reputation as a hard man. As an old Norfolk rhyme attests: 'There never was a Paston poor, or a Heydon a coward.'

He clashed with the Pastons, taking Lord Moleyns' side against them in the dispute over Gresham Castle (see page 54). He also clashed with the Pastons' patron Sir John Falstolf, because he backed Falstolf's opponents in disputes over property. However, he managed to survive the Wars of the Roses, despite his enemies' attempts to have him arraigned for 'riding against the statute'.

Heydon's marriage was unhappy, and he believed that his wife Eleanor had been unfaithful, to the point where he refused to recognise her second child and named only his first child, Henry, in his will. Margaret Paston reported that John threatened to cut off Eleanor's nose (presumably to show the world that she was an adulteress) and to kill the child if they came anywhere near him – and later he was accused of 'putting away of his wife and keeping another'.

Sir John Heydon died from the plague in 1479/80, and his son Henry Heydon completed the house by around 1486 – just before Henry VII passed laws which stopped private houses being fortified. Baconsthorpe Castle, despite its grand name, was actually more of a fortified manor than a castle. The inner gatehouse and curtain wall were equipped for artillery during the Wars of the Roses, and there is a keyhole gun port in the north wall. The house was also moated, with a drawbridge. John Leland, writing in 1540, said that, 'Henry son of John Heydon performed with an exceeding cost the [w]hole house, whereof John Heydon began only the front.'

Henry Heydon was knighted by Henry VII at his coronation. Like his father, Henry was a lawyer and JP. He died in 1503/4, leaving eight children – the eldest of whom, John II, inherited the Norfolk estates.

Murder, astrology, legal disputes and duels

Sir John Heydon II was a great courtier with a very lavish lifestyle. He was created Knight of the Bath at the coronation of Henry VIII and apparently settled down to become a model citizen. He converted the east range of the house into a wool-processing shed during the sixteenth century. His son, Sir Christopher Heydon,

Baconsthorpe Castle.

inherited the hall in 1550 and added the turreted outer gatehouse and the outer court. Sir Christopher was also noted for his charity and fairness, and it was said that he entertained thirty 'master-shepherds' of his own flocks for one Christmas dinner.

William Heydon was the next to succeed to Baconsthorpe. He and his eldest son Christopher were the ones who wrought the family's downfall, as both of them were hot-tempered and clashed extremely badly. Christopher lived at Saxlingham Hall with his wife Lady Mirabel; allegedly, a serving maid was killed there and the blood left an indelible red spot on the stairs. (The legend of blood that can't be scrubbed away is found elsewhere in Norfolk – see Thetford Nunnery, page 133.)

William was forced to mortgage Baconsthorpe to satisfy his creditors, and in 1590 he decided to sell the castle. Christopher pointed out that he couldn't actually do that, because the property was entailed; his father, furious at being baulked, threatened to demolish the castle instead. Christopher went straight to the Privy Council, who told William he was not allowed to demolish the house; they added that William's behaviour was unnatural and would set a bad example. Legal disputes ensued, and they dragged on for years.

Lady Mirabel died in 1593 at the age of 32, and Christopher built her a massive tomb in the shape of an Egyptian pyramid in the chancel of Saxlingham church. Christopher was deeply interested in astronomy and covered the pyramid in hieroglyphics and astrological signs. These 'strange signs' may have given rise to the legend that Lady Mirabel's ghost rode nightly from Saxlingham to Bayfield Hall, though her reasons for the journey haven't survived with the legend. The pyramid eventually became unsafe and was removed in 1789; but Lady Mirabel's alabaster image, kneeling on a cushion, survived and is still in a niche in the church.

Lady Mirabel.

Perhaps Mirabel's death meant that Christopher felt he had nothing left to lose, and he took his father to court over the entailment issue in 1593. When William died in 1594 and left his property to his wife, Christopher promptly took his mother to court, suing her for the castle. His mother appealed to Elizabeth I and eventually the dispute was settled, with Christopher owing £11,000 in debts he'd inherited from his father to add to his own debts of £3,000 (a total of £14,000 – equivalent to over £2 million in modern money).

It's hardly surprising that Christopher needed money – and fast. He joined the Earl of Essex in sacking Cadiz in 1586, where Essex knighted him. Although Christopher remarried in 1599, the marriage didn't settle his debts or his temper, and he challenged Sir John Townshend to a duel in 1600. The Privy Council managed to stop the duel, but when Christopher's brother John – an equally hot-headed man – challenged Sir Robert Mansell to a duel later that year, the Privy Council was unable to stop it happening. John's hand was chopped off, and rather gruesomely became an exhibit in Canterbury museum!

Christopher was forced to mortgage Baconsthorpe, and his influence in the county had declined so much that he couldn't prevent Robert Mansell's election to Parliament. The Heydons promptly joined their patron Essex's rebellion in February 1601 – and when it all backfired, John escaped to the Netherlands and

Christopher went into hiding while he negotiated a truce with Sir Robert Cecil. He offered to pay a fine, but pointed out that he already had huge debts, as well as fourteen children to support. He was imprisoned in the Fleet, but he was released and pardoned when he paid a fine of £2,000 (which was still an awful lot of money to find – it's equivalent to £290,000 in today's money).

He was just as combative in his intellectual life; John Chamber had called for astrology to be outlawed in a treatise of 1601, and Christopher wrote *A Defence of Judiciall Astrologie* in 1603, an enormous treatise which argued that astronomy was a valid science and religiously sound. Nobody challenged his arguments for the next 20 years; and in the meantime Christopher wrote treatises on astronomy, including comets. In 1603, he wrote a letter to a friend saying that the eclipse of 1605 could predict 'a new Democraty or Aristocraty of the Church and Commonwealth': highly interesting, considering that the seventeenth century gave rise to the Civil War and a change in the commonwealth.

The decline of the castle

Sir Christopher died in 1624. Despite mortgaging the rest of his estates, he was still in debt. His eldest son, William, drowned on a military expedition at La Rochelle in 1627; his second son, John, was a noted mathematician and court wit, who became the lieutenant of the ordnance and was knighted in 1629. However, John chose the wrong side in the Civil War: he was the lieutenant-general in charge of supplying Charles I's artillery. John's lands were seized in 1642 and, although he was allowed to buy them back, the family continued to be deeply in debt.

After John's death in 1653, his son (also named John) followed the family tradition by becoming a lawyer and astrologer; he was put in prison in 1657 for foretelling Cromwell's death. Despite the fact that he was a Royalist, John was thrown into jail again in 1663 by Charles II for 'seditious practices' – and yet again four years later, when he and the duke of Buckingham were accused of plotting against the king. John had apparently predicted the date of the king's death; however, he claimed that he was innocent and the case was eventually dropped. He wrote several books on alchemy and mysticism, but wrote nothing after 1670 – and how and when he died is unknown.

What we do know is that the family was desperate for money and ended up demolishing most of the castle and selling the stone, some of which ended up at Felbrigg Hall. The remains of the castle was sold to merchant Daniel Bridges in 1673. Ten years later, the property was sold to a doctor called Zurishaddai Lang, and finally it was bought by the Mott family in the early 1800s. The gatehouse, which had been used as a house, collapsed in 1920, and the building was left to decay.

In 1940, Charles Mott-Radclyffe gave the castle to the Ministry of Public Buildings and Works (now English Heritage). Nowadays the castle is open to the public; there is no charge.

Priory of St Mary in the Meadow, Beeston Regis

The priory of St Mary in the Meadow lies on a track near Abbey Farm, just off the Cromer Road in Beeston Regis (OS map reference TG 167 427). It's open to the public during daylight hours.

It was an Augustinian friary, which was founded by Margaret de Caiesneto (aka Margaret de Cressy) around 1216, and was dedicated to St Mary. It was dissolved in June 1539, with three religious people 'of good name', seven servants and six children. The church and cloisters are in ruins, although one building was converted to a house; there are two surviving fishponds and some earthworks.

Scandals

For most of the time, life was peaceful at Beeston, but there were two notable moments of trouble.

The first was in 1317, when John de Walsam, one of the canons of Beeston, had a serious row with the Bishop of Norwich. The cause of the row is lost to history, but the results are well documented – de Walsam attacked the bishop with a sword and wounded him. De Walsam was sent to Rome to explain himself to the pope; and in December 1317 Pope John XXII told the bishop to 'enjoin penance and satisfaction' on the canon, as he had given the canon absolution.

Beeston Priory.

Beeston Priory.

The second time the priory fell foul of the authorities was on 25 August 1494, when Bishop Goldwell visited and the prior was forced to admit that there was only one other canon in the priory – a man called Thomas Taverner, who had gone absent without leave. Goldwell told the canon that he had to get two more canons as soon as possible, and to do the accounts annually. Twenty years later, Bishop Nix did another visitation – and Thomas Taverner was still missing! This time, he was reported to be celebrating Mass in Norwich, but the bishop let it lie.

Confusion and dissolution

Lord Morley wrote to Cromwell in March 1537 asking for the priory, saying that he'd been a patron and heard that the priory was going to be suppressed. It was another year before Sir Richard Rich wrote to Cromwell saying that he was going to suppress Beeston – and that the inmates 'pretended to be friars' but were actually canons. Although the house was typical of a small house of Austin Canons, it was described in the Episcopal registers as a hospital of canons; in the patent rolls, it was described as a priory of Carmelite friars, so there was clearly some confusion about what the establishment at Beeston actually was.

The monks' fishpond from Beeston Priory.

However, it didn't manage to escape the reformers; it was dissolved in June 1539. Prior Hudson was given a pension of £5, and became the rector of Newton Flotman. John Travers was granted the lease of the priory, and finally in 1545 the site was granted jointly to Sir Edmund Wyndham and Giles Seafoule.

The priory and the hooded grey ghost

In the 1930s to 1940s it was reported that there were two boulders on the edge of a footpath running through the priory grounds; so the story goes, a hooded grey ghost hid behind them and leapt out at passers-by at sunset. A local farmer, James Reynolds (born in 1857), used to drive his horses through the path and the ghost terrified his horses. Annoyed and wanting to put the apparition to rest, Reynolds suggested that one of the stones should be put on top of his own grave when he died, so the ghost would no longer have a hiding place. He died in 1941 and the stone was placed on his grave – and the ghost apparently was never seen again after that.

Gravestone of James Reynolds and his wife Ann at All Saints Church, Beeston Regis.

Tunnels and treasure

As with many of the religious houses in Norfolk, Beeston Priory has a claim to a subterranean tunnel; apparently, it ran to the Dunstable Arms Inn on the Cromer Road. However, no trace of the tunnel has been found.

J. Cox, writing in *Norfolk Notes and Queries* in 1885, says that the tunnel from the priory runs in a different direction: firstly to the wayside cross at Gresham, and from there to Gresham Castle. And somewhere hidden in the tunnel is an image like a calf, made of gold. Allegedly, in the 1820s, an old lady who lived a quarter of a mile from the cross decided to excavate her property to see if she could find the golden calf. She dug a hole in her parlour floor (which presumably was of beaten earth) and 'hundreds of barrowloads' of soil were excavated. She didn't find the golden calf – but, when her excavations threatened to undermine the house next door, belonging to Admiral Luken of Felbrigg Hall, she was forced to stop looking.

And the calf?

It still hasn't been found.

Binham Priory

Binham Priory is just off the Warham Road in Beeston (OS map reference TG 982 399). The remains of the twelfth-century Benedictine priory are the most complete monastic ruins in Norfolk, and are open to the public; the church is still in use as the parish church.

The beginnings of the priory

The priory was founded in 1091 by Peter de Valoines, a nephew of William the Conqueror, and his wife Albreda, although its charter dates from 1104. It took more than a century to build the abbey, and the stone was brought in from Barnack in Northamptonshire. The priory was a cell of the monastery at St Albans and was dedicated to the Honour of the Blessed Virgin (i.e. St Mary). Eight monks from St Albans were to live at Binham, and on St Alban's day they had to pay a silver mark to the abbey of St Albans. Under the terms of the charter, the abbot of St Albans was allowed to visit, but only for eight days (unless the prior invited him to stay for longer) and he wasn't allowed to bring more than thirteen horses with him.

Binham Priory.

The Siege of Fitzwalter

There was a huge row in 1212 when the abbot of St Albans removed Prior Thomas from office. Thomas's friend, the baron Robert Fitzwalter, claimed that he had a deed from St Albans which said the Abbot of St Albans couldn't remove a prior of Binham without the consent of the patron – and Fitzwalter added that he was the patron and definitely didn't consent to Prior Thomas's removal. He promptly took the abbot of St Albans to the king's court. His claims against the abbot included that the abbot had come to the priory of Binham to lodge there with more men and horses than he was meant to have by the original agreement; he'd increased the number of monks from St Albans living there, again in contravention of the original agreement; and he'd forced the men of Binham to

Binham Priory.

give him much more than the silver mark per year that they'd agreed to pay.

Whether the allegations against the abbot were true or not, Fitzwalter had lied about being the patron of the priory – his deed was forged. He duly lost the case, and retaliated by putting the priory under siege by his retainers, so the monks inside could only get rainwater to drink and could only make bread from bran.

King John was furious, saying, 'Ho, by God's feet, either I or Fitzwalter must be King of England!' He sent armed forces under the command of Norfolk man John Grey to protect the priory, and Fitzwalter fled the kingdom. Until his death, Fitzwalter still claimed that he was the patron of Binham. However, when Fitzwalter died, his friend and fellow soldier Adam Fitzwilliam retrieved the forged deed and gave it to the abbot of St Albans. Fitzwilliam also gave the abbot a silver cup, to make up for his share in the offence.

King John's verdict, when it was all over, was, 'Ho! By God's feet, who ever heard of such things in peaceable times in a Christian land?'

The scandal of William the alchemist

The discord between Binham and St Albans rumbled on, and came to a head in 1318. The prior at Binham, William de Somerton, was very keen on the pursuit of alchemy – the so-called science of being able to turn base metal into gold. To fund his researches, he sold a quantity of the priory's belongings – including two chalices, six copes (large capes with deep collars worn in processions), three chasubles (a priest's outer vestments), seven gold rings, silk clothes, silver cups and spoons, a silver cup and the crown in which the Host was suspended before the altar. Hugh, the Abbot of St Albans, wanted his usual silver mark on St Alban's day – and because de Somerton had spent all the money on his laboratory, he couldn't afford to pay the silver mark, or to buy food for the monks.

A huge row erupted, and de Somerton asked the Sheriff of Norfolk to send a force to stop the abbot of St Albans going to the priory. Meanwhile, the abbot appealed to the Edward II, who ordered the Sheriff of Norfolk to withdraw. The abbot sacked William, but William refused to leave the house – and clearly he was popular, because his monks supported him.

At the general chapter of the Benedictines of Canterbury Province in Northampton, the abbot of Ramsey told the king that the monks at Binham were disobedient, insolent and had taken up arms against the abbot of St Albans. He asked the king for help. The king came down on the side of the abbot, and in October 1320 he ordered the Sheriff of Norfolk to arrest de Somerton and thirteen monks at Binham.

De Somerton said that the allegations were untrue and appealed to Rome, and in 1321 Pope John XXII wrote to Edward II to say he'd heard Binham's side of the story. Allegedly a messenger and notary delivered letters of commission from the king's chaplain to the abbot of St Albans, and they had been beaten so hard that 'blood sprinkled the walls of the church'. The monks who protested at this bad treatment of the messengers and appealed to the pope were kept in prison without food for six days. The pope wanted the archbishop of Canterbury to look into the matter – and he said that if the monks at Binham were telling the truth, the abbot of St Albans had to come to Rome to explain himself. The king's reply was that it was a pack of lies – bad men were trying to get the abbot of St Albans into trouble – and he asked for the pope's support.

In 1322 the king put two custodians into the priory of Binham: William de Leycester, a clerk, and Nicholas de Flamstede, a monk of St Albans. De Somerton fled, the situation appeared to improve, and in 1323 the king told his custodians not to interfere any longer in the affairs at Binham. Later that year, Nicholas de Flamstede was appointed prior at Binham, and after that things seemed to settle down.

Mad monks – and bad omens

One of the saddest stories at Binham was that of Alexander de Langley, the one-time prior of Wymondham and Keeper of the Abbot's Seal at St Albans. He went insane through studying too much and was prone to outbursts of frenzy. He was flogged by the Abbot of St Albans, and when that didn't restore his sanity he was kept in solitary confinement in the west gate (also known as the Gaol Gate) at Binham from 1224 until his death, when he was buried in chains on the north side of the churchyard.

Binham played a part in the Rising (aka Peasants' Revolt) of 1381; on 20 June, John Lister, a Binham man, led the revolt and burned the priory's records. It was reasonably quiet at the priory from then until 1454, when Henry Halstede, a monk of St Albans who'd been prior at Wymondham Abbey, asked to be made prior of Binham. Halstede promised to clear the priory's debts and rebuild the ruined dorter – but the monks at Binham knew of Henry's reputation as a troublemaker and refused to have him as their prior. The abbot said that the monks were self-willed and reminded them that the Christian religion meant forgiving people, and Henry got his way.

Halstede's successor in 1461 also ended up in trouble; William Dixwell was eccentric, and tended to wander about like a vagabond. He was deposed in 1464 and replaced by John Peyton, but then reappointed in 1465 (possibly after having served as abbot at Wymondham). There is another gap in 1480 when Richard Whitingdon was named as prior; it's possible that Dixwell went wandering again, but then he was reappointed in 1481 until his death in 1502.

Leyton and Legh visited in 1536 and claimed that three of the monks were incontinent (in other words, they didn't keep their vow of celibacy). However, when the county commissioners visited, they didn't say that any of the monks were particularly bad.

The priory was suppressed in May 1539. The property was granted to Thomas Paxton, whose grandson Edward intended to pull the building down and build himself a house on the site. However, when work started, one of the walls fell down, killing a workman. His fellow labourers, seeing it as a bad omen, flatly refused to continue the work, and Paxton had to give up; the house was eventually built at Appleton instead.

Spooks: Jimmy the Fiddler and the Black Monk

At some time in the 1600s, a hole opened up by the priory; it was thought to be the result of a tunnel collapsing. Nobody was brave enough to go near it until Jimmy Griggs the fiddler said that he and his dog Trap would explore it. He said that he would go into the tunnel and play his fiddle so everyone on the surface could follow him by the music and know exactly where he was.

The plan worked until, at Fiddler's Hill, the music stopped.

Trap reappeared with his tail between his legs, shivering with terror – but Jimmy Griggs was never seen again. There was a bad storm that night, and the villagers were all convinced that Jimmy had been taken by the Black Monk, a figure said to haunt the grounds of the priory. The Black Monk apparently emerged from a tunnel linking Binham with Walsingham.

In April 1935, the road was widened and cut through the north side of Fiddler's Hill, which was actually a round barrow. Workmen found human bones and the skeleton of a small animal; everyone thought of Jimmy Griggs. However, archaeologists said that it was unlikely there had been a tunnel from the priory, because it would have had to cross the path of a stream – besides which, the bones were from a Saxon burial ground, hundreds of years before the priory's foundation, let alone its dissolution.

Blackborough Priory

The remains of the twelfth-century Blackborough Priory is simply part of a wall of a barn in Priory Farm off Wormegay Road in Blackborough End, near Middleton (OS map reference TF 673 140). It is not open to the public.

Beginnings of the priory

Blackborough itself was originally known as Shiplade; according to the eighteenth-century historian Francis Blomefield it was 'low, fenny ground'.The priory was founded in about 1135 by Roger de Scales and his wife Muriel, dedicated to the honour of the Blessed Virgin (i.e. St Mary) and St Catherine. Originally the house was just for monks; then Roger's son extended it so that nuns could live there as well ('*sororibus et fratribus*'). In 1200 it became a nunnery and was a Benedictine house; by 1291 there were forty-four nuns and servants living there, as well as people in the guest house.

The nuns ran into financial difficulties in 1347 and Edward III let them off taxation for two years. Clearly they managed to keep going, because all was reported well at Bishop Nix's visitation of 1514 – with the exception of the church porch being in ruins, and the prioress didn't give annual accounts to avoid paying an auditor. The visitation of 1520 reported that all was well, and the visitation of 1532 said that all was well apart from the house being in need of repairs.

Dissolution and after

Although Legh and Leyton's comperta of 1536 claimed that Prioress Dawney and two of her nuns were 'incontinent' (in other words, they didn't keep their vow of celibacy), the report of 1537 presented a completely different picture: it said that there were 'nine religious persons of good name and fame' in the priory.

The priory was suppressed in March 1537 – though Richard Southwell wryly wrote to Cromwell that the nuns had taken as much as they could with them as they left the priory, so there was nothing left to pay their debts of £79 (the equivalent of just over £32,000 in modern terms).

Very little is left of the building now, but excavations have shown interesting finds – including, in 1834, a 7-foot-tall skeleton in a stone coffin.

A medieval love story

One of the great medieval love stories was played out partly at Blackborough Priory. When Margery Paston was about 18 years old, she fell in love with Richard Calle, the family's bailiff, who was almost twice her age.

The Pastons found out about the love affair in about May 1469 – after Mr Lovell had asked Margery's brother John (known as John III, to distinguish him from his elder brother John II) a couple of times if he 'understood how it was between R. C. and [John's] sister' because his oldest son knew of a good marriage for her. John Paston III was incredibly upset, because the family wanted Margery to marry a social superior rather than their landless servant. Richard Calle's family were shopkeepers – wealthy shopkeepers, admittedly, but they didn't have enough social cachet for the Pastons, who had only recently become part of the gentry. Margery's actions threatened their good name. John III wrote to his brother John II in disgust:

> I answered him that if my father … were alive and had consented to it, and my mother and you both, he should never have my good will to make my sister sell candles and mustard at Framlingham.

This was an unfair gibe because Richard had no intention of being a merchant. He knew French and Latin, and he was very capable of dealing with business affairs; the Pastons really needed him to negotiate leases with tenants, collect rentals, keep accounts and attend legal hearings on behalf of the family. He was also an accomplished letter-writer, he was religiously devout, and the Pastons had relied on him for years.

Knowing that the family didn't approve of their relationship, Richard and Margery married in secret. And when Margaret Paston found out what had happened, she demanded that her wayward daughter should renounce her new husband. Margery refused, and Margaret made sure that they were parted – Richard was kept in London and Margery was kept in her mother's house.

Although the Pastons suspected Richard of pushing Margery into the betrothal for his own ends, he clearly loved her, and one of his letters to her survives (despite the fact that he asked her to burn it):

> My own lady and mistress, and before God my true wife, I with heart full sorrowful recommend me to you, as he that cannot be merry nor shall be until it be otherwise with us than it is yet; for this life that we lead now is no pleasure to God or to the world, considering the great bond of matrimony that is made between us, and also the great love that has been and I trust yet is between us, and on my part never greater. Wherefore I beseech Almighty God to comfort us as soon as it pleases Him, for we that ought by right to be most together are most asunder; it seems a thousand years ago since I spoke with you. I had rather be with you than have all the goods in the world. Alas, alas! good lady, they remember full little what they do that keep us thus asunder.

There were no witnesses to the marriage; at the time, church law meant that if the promises had been made and the marriage consummated, the union was irrevocable. (Divorce – although clearly John II had suggested it to his mother, judging by her reaction in a letter – was seen as the kind of sin that ended in hellfire and damnation.) But if the Pastons could persuade Margery to say she hadn't made the vows, the marriage could be declared illegal. At the time, the Pastons had other worries – they'd just been besieged at Caister (see page 29). So Margery's rebellion came at a particularly difficult time for the Pastons.

Margery was put in solitary confinement. However, she had the example of her aunt Elizabeth who, when in her late teens, was supposed to be betrothed to Stephen Scrope, 'an old battered widower of nearly 50', and refused. Elizabeth was kept in isolation and also beaten every day, but she refused to give in.

Margery, too, refused to give in.

On 8 September 1469, Margaret and Margery's grandmother Agnes took Margery to William Lyhart, the Bishop of Norwich, to be interrogated; Margaret wrote a very detailed account of it to John II. The Bishop of Norwich reminded Margery of her genteel station, her family and friends, and 'what rebuke and shame and loss it should be to her' if she were not guided by them. He'd heard that she 'loved such one as her friends were not pleased with that she should have' and wanted to know exactly what she'd said to Calle, so he could determine 'whether it made matrimony or not'. Margery's response angered her mother still further:

> And she rehearsed what she had said, and said if those words made it not sure, she said boldly that she would make it surer before she went thence; for she said she thought in her conscience she was bound, what so ever the words were. These lewd words grieved me and her grand-dam as much as all the remnant.

The bishop also interrogated Richard Calle separately and discovered that his story tallied exactly with Margery's. Clearly wanting to give the Pastons a chance to 'find other things against him that might cause the letting hereof' (i.e. manufacture some evidence to make the marriage illegal), the bishop said he 'would not be too hasty' to deliver judgement and would leave it until the Wednesday after Michaelmas – which meant they had to wait for a whole month.

Meanwhile, Margaret banned Margery from the family home and refused to receive her. The Bishop of Norwich intervened and sent her to stay with Roger Best, a grocer who was also the sheriff of Norwich. Margery wrote to John that she was sorry that the Bests had been 'acumbered with her', but at least Best's 'sadness and good disposition' meant that Margery 'shall not be suffered there to play the brethel [sic]' (i.e. be treated as a whore … or entertain Richard Calle).

Margaret was still insistent that Margery would 'full sore repent her lewdness hereafter' – but clearly that wasn't the case and, in the end, the bishop upheld the marriage. Richard took a job as the receiver at Blackborough Priory, and Margery joined him there; they had a public marriage and settled down together. Calle bought an estate at Bacton, and they had three sons togeher.

The Pastons discovered they really couldn't do without their estate manager and reinstated him in 1472, although he was never accepted as part of the family. Despite the fact that Margaret had written during the dispute that 'even if he were dead at this hour, [Margery] should never be in my heart as she was', clearly she unbent to some degree because at her death in 1484 she left £20 (equivalent to just over £8,000 in modern terms) in her will to John, Margery's eldest child by Richard. Although she left nothing to Margery, it's possible that Margery had died by this point (Calle remarried); but Margaret made her point and left absolutely nothing in her will to her son-in-law.

Bromholm Priory

Bromholm Priory – also known as Bacton Abbey, although it was never actually an abbey! – lies on the boundary of modern-day Bacton, just through the remains of the gatehouse on Abbey Street (OS map reference TG 349 331). It's on private land and isn't open to the public.

The beginnings of the priory

The priory was an offshoot from the Cluniac priory at Castle Acre (see page 32) and was founded in 1113 by William de Glanville. The priory was dedicated to St Andrew and the buildings and church were originally made from wood; there was enough room for seven or eight monks to live and work there, and it acted as a staging post on the pilgrim route to Walsingham.

Gateway to Bromholm Priory.

The priory was very poor, but its fortunes changed swiftly in 1223, when it came into the possession of a piece of the True Cross. As a result, many pilgrims visited and gave enough money and gifts to replace the wooden structures on the site with stone buildings. Henry III was a frequent visitor; in 1229 he granted the priory a fair on Holy Cross Day and the two days after (i.e. 14–17 September), and a Monday market. In 1233 he gave the priory a silver model of a ship, and the following year he gave them a silver-gilt image of himself.

He wasn't the only royal benefactor; Edward II visited in 1313 and granted the priory the manor of Bacton, worth £12 9s and 7¼d a year (equivalent to over £5,000 in modern terms).

The Cross of Bromholm

According to the thirteenth-century chronicler Matthew Paris – a monk at the abbey of St Albans – Baldwin, the Emperor of Constantinople, owned a piece of the the cross on which Christ was crucified. Paris described the cross as 'two pieces of wood, placed one across the other, and almost as wide as the hand of a man'. The pieces were supposedly from the places where Christ's hands and feet were nailed to the wood, so they were therefore soaked in holy blood. The cross had been found by St Helen, the mother of the Roman emperor Constantine, during a visit to Jerusalem in the early fourth century, and she gave part of the cross to Constantine. The cross was passed down through the emperors, who took it into battle with them to make sure that they were kept safe and victorious.

However, in 1205, the emperor Baldwin forgot to take the cross with him and was captured; he was killed, the following year. Hugh, the clergyman who served in Baldwin's chapel, realised that trouble lay ahead, so he took all the relics from the chapel – including the cross – and fled to England. There, he toured around various monasteries, offering the relics with the condition that if Hugh let them have the True Cross, he and his two sons should be admitted to that particular priory as monks. (This must have taken quite some time, because it was nearly 20 years after he fled to England that the cross arrived at Bromholm.)

The abbot at St Albans was quite happy to buy two fingers of St Margaret from the clergyman, but didn't believe that the cross was genuine. Eventually, Hugh reached Bromholm – where, according to Paris, 'the monks were overjoyed to have such a treasure'. They promptly used it for miraculous cures – including leprosy, lameness, possession by devils and even, according to the fifteenth-century chronicler John Capgrave, restoring 39 dead people to life as well as curing 19 people of blindness.

The cross's fame soon spread, and it's even referenced in medieval literature. In Langland's *Vision of Piers Plowman*, there are the lines:

> And bidde the Roode of Bromholm,
> Bryng me out of dette.

And in Chaucer's *The Reeve's Tale* there is a plea for help by the miller's wife:

> Helpe, holy cross of Bromeholme.

Matthew Paris added darkly that 'some, their sins it is supposed being the cause, are unable to look perfectly upon the said piece, thereby sometimes incurring infirmities of divers sorts'. Although to modern eyes it's unbelieveable that a little piece of wood could cure someone from an ailment, belief in the cross acted as a placebo; modern medicine recognises that around 30 per cent of clinical test patients improve simply because they believe that they're doing something to help, and it's likely that some of the symptoms of the medieval petitioners were improved in the same way.

During the fifteenth century, the monks sold visitors small pictures of the Rood – a double cross with a little crucifix figure – to help boost the abbey's income.

So what happened to the cross? John Foxe, in his *Book of Martyrs*, says that Hugh Pie, the chaplain of Ludney, was brought before bishop of Norwich in July 1424 for saying that people shouldn't go on pilgrimages or worship crosses or other images, and he'd also cast the cross of Bromholm into the fire. However, Pie denied the charges, and had three priests and three laymen as his witnesses. It's clear that he burned one of the pictures rather than the actual cross, because the cross was mentioned in the visitation of 1536 (along with the girdle and milk of the Virgin, and pieces of the crosses of Saint Peter and Saint Andrew). In 1537, Richard Southwell wrote to Cromwell that he had charge of the cross. On 26 February, he wrote that he had delivered the cross to Robert Codde (the former

Bromholm Priory.

prior of Pentney, who became Warden of the Great Hospital in Norwich), to give to Cromwell. Presumably it was sold, as the Bromholm Cross isn't mentioned after that date.

Fight for supremacy

Shortly after the arrival of the cross, in 1225, the prior died and a new prior had to be appointed. The priory of Castle Acre claimed that, as Bromholm was subject to them, they should elect its prior. Bromholm immediately petitioned the Pope for the right to elect their own prior. The row continued for four years, and finally Gregory IX referred judgement to the abbot of Olveston and the deans of Rutland and Stamford. The abbot said that when a vacancy for the prior occurred, Castle Acre should nominate three of their own monks and three from Bromholm, and Bromholm should then choose one of these six as prior. Prior Vincent was duly elected – but there were still grumbles as, ten years later, Vincent wrote to Cluny about differences between Bromholm and Castle Acre.

By 1385, despite the riches gained through offerings to the Cross of Bromholm, the priory was in financial trouble. Several of their properties and a proprtion of their land had been 'wasted by the sea', they'd suffered badly with 'pestilence' (i.e. the plague), and there had been a large fire at the priory. They were near the point of closure, but begged the pope for help. Boniface IX gave them leave to hear confessions and grant absolution to pilgrims who came to see the cross, as well as giving them an indulgence to receive alms from penitents and giving them the livings of several churches.

The fake prior

And then another row blew up over the ruler of the priory in the early fifteenth century. Prior Clement Chandellier resigned his office, and the monks had chosen

Nicholas to succeed him as prior, but in April 1418 the pope deposed Nicholas in favour of a man called John Paston. Paston claimed that he was kin to the Pastons of Paston Hall; but William Paston said that it was a complete fabrication and John Paston's real name was John Wortes – he wasn't in any way part of the Paston family. (However, it seems that he was originally a monk from Bromholm.)

Chandellier accused John Paston of apostasy and took control of the priory again. There were two forms of apostasy in England, so apostasy meant either renouncing your faith or, if you were a professed religious person, leaving the religious life for a secular one without permission, so the form of apostasy was probably the latter. Chandellier was backed by his legal counsel, a local judge – who just so happened to be William Paston.

John took the fight to Rome, who came down on his side. The Roman court told Chandellier to resign and fined William Paston £205 (the equivalent of about £84,000 in today's money). Against the advice of his friends, William protested – and the pope promptly excommunicated him.

In 1426, John Paston was appointed as the Bishop of Cork. William Paston referred to him as 'this cursed Bishop of Bromholm' and pointed out that the bishopric of Cork wasn't actually vacant so John couldn't be appointed to it. Finally, in 1430, John Paston resigned from Bromholm. He hadn't lived there for several years or performed his duties as prior. William Paston wrote to the abbot of Cluny, saying that several 'virtuous men' who dressed as monks had lived at the priory for nine or ten years but were still 'unprofessed' (i.e. they hadn't taken their vows), and asking if the prior of Thetford could come and sort it out.

A funeral fit for a king

Sir John Paston, the son of Judge William Paston, died in London on 21 or 22 May 1446, and his funeral was held at Bromholm on 29 May 1446. Part of the delay was obviously caused by having to bring the body from London to Norfolk, but the monks put the time to good use, planning a very lavish funeral – and also engaging a barber for five days to help smarten them up.

One London chandler was paid £5, 19 shillings and 4 pence for candles, and another chandler was paid 55 shillings and 11¼ pence (between them, this was the equivalent of over £5,000, in terms of today's money – an astoundingly large sum for candles), and plenty of additional candles were bought from local chandlers. A glazier was paid 20 shillings to take out two of the windows in the church 'to let out the reek of the torches' – basically, to stop the congregation suffocating! – and then put the windows back again.

There was an incredible amount of food and drink, including 13 barrels of beer, 27 barrels of ale, 15 gallons of wine, 41 pigs, 49 calves, 1,300 eggs, 20 gallons of milk and 8 gallons of cream. £5, 13 shillings and 4 pence was spent as a dole to the poor (interestingly, much less than was spent on candles!), and £20 in gold was changed into small coins to shower among the attendant throng. But money was also given to local churches, including those of Bacton, Paston and Gresham, and also to Reedham church whose steeple needed huge repairs.

Spooks, prophecies and tunnels

There is one ghost story associated with the priory; the beach is said to be haunted by a monk, who found a girl washed there by the storm. When she died, he apparently died of a broken heart and now he walks the beach, trying to find her.

There was also a saying about the monastery:

When Keswic church becomes a barn,
Broomholme Abbey will be a farm.

Back in 1842, Charles Green noted that there was a barn on the site of the old church belonging to Mr W. Sturgess, and the priory was a farm occupied by Mr W. Cubitt. It seems that the prophecy came true.

In common with several of the other monastic buildings in the county, there's a legend about a subterranean tunnel. The tunnel at Bacton apparently runs to Gimingham Hall, about four miles away, and in the middle of the tunnel there's a pair of huge golden gates. So far, nobody has found any evidence of a tunnel, let alone golden gates.

The end of the priory

Thomas Cromwell, Henry VIII's vice-regent, asked three lawyers in ecclesiastical orders to carry out a visitation or enquiry to all the religious orders, after the execution of Sir Thomas More in 1535, and to report back. Dr Thomas Legh and Dr Richard Leyton carried out most of the visitations, as they were younger than Dr John Ap Rice and much travelling was involved. However, their reports tended to differ markedly from what the bishop had found in his own ecclesiastical visitations, and from what the king's county commissioners (in the case of Norfolk, led by Sir Richard Cromwell) said about the institutions and their inmates. It's highly likely that Legh, Leyton and Ap Rice focused on the bad points of each house (and exaggerated many of them), as the good points of the houses were ignored – and this was exactly what Cromwell needed as evidence to suppress the monasteries and annexe their property for the king.

In Bromholm's case, the visitation was in 1536. Legh and Leyton claimed that Prior Lakenham and three monks confessed to being 'incontinent' (in other words, they didn't keep their vow of celibacy). However, the county commissioners also visited the priory and stated that there were four religious persons there, all 'of very good name and fame', along with four servants, three almoners and twenty-six labourers. The house was in good repair, with the bells and lead worth £200, a hundred acres of woodland worth just over £66, and cattle, corn and moveable goods worth £49. The monastery was dissolved in February 1537, and Prior Lakenham was given a pension of 20 marks.

Burgh Castle

Burgh Castle is the remains of one of the third-century Roman shore forts; there is a Norman earthwork motte and bailey castle within the fort, and it's also thought to be the location of St Fursey's monastery in the seventh century.

The site is in the care of the Norfolk Archaeological Trust, and is located in the fields behind the church at Church Road, Burgh Castle – roughly two miles west of Yarmouth (map reference TG 475 045), overlooking Breydon Water. The site is open to the public.

The Roman shore fort

There were eleven shore forts stretching between Brancaster and Porchester (Hampshire), which protected the coastline against pirates, raids or invasions. Burgh Castle was known as 'Gariannonum'. The garrison there included some of the Stablesian cavalry from Greece, who were trained in marsh warfare and were regarded as an elite rapid-response troop.

Three sides of the original Roman walls remain, and they're an incredible eight feet thick and fifteen feet high. The west wall collapsed and fell into the Waveney well before the eighteenth century, when it was described by local historian John Ives. The walls enclose an area of between six and seven acres.

William Camden described the site in his *Britannica*:

> We call it at this day **Burgh-Castle**. Which, as Beda saith, was *a most pleasant Castle by reason of woods and sea together, wherein a Monastery was built by Fursaey a holy Scot*, by whose perswasion Sigebert King of the East-Angles became a Monke and resigned up his Kingdome: who afterwards, being drawne against his will out of this Monastery to encourage his people in battaile against the Mercians, together with his company lost his life. In that place now there are onely ruinous wals in forme, as it were, foure square, built of flint stone and British Bricke, but all overgrown with briers and bushes: among which otherwhiles are Romane peeces of coins gotten foorth, so that it may seeme to have been one of those fortifications that the Romans placed upon the river Yare to represse the piracies of the Saxons, or rather that it was the ancient Garianonum it selfe, where the Stablesian Horsmen had their Station and kept ward at the declination of the Romane Empire in Britaine.

In 1756 a five-feet-square trench was opened in the field next to the castle, which was believed to be the burial ground of the garrison. In the trench, archaeologists found many fragments of urns; one fragment also contained coins from Constantine's reign, bones, ashes and the head of a Roman spear.

Burgh Castle.

St Fursey

St Fursey was an Irish monk known for his trances and visions. Bede's description of St Fursey's vision of the afterlife is one of the earliest of its kind, describing angels and devils, and it's thought that Dante drew on them when writing his *Divine Comedy*. St Fursey became a missionary and came to Norfolk in 630 – the first known missionary in the county. King Sigebert gave him the fortress of Cnobheresburg (i.e. Burgh Castle) and Fursey built a monastery there. When Sigebert was killed in battle against Penda, the king of Mercia, Fursey travelled to France.

The Normans

When the Normans arrived, they built a castle in the south-west corner of the fort. It was levelled in the eighteenth century and the last traces of the motte were destroyed in 1839 – although it's still visible in crop marks.

Ghostly encounters

On 27 April, just before dawn, it's said that you can hear the sound of clashing swords and the screams of Roman and Saxon soldiers in battle. There's also a legend that on misty May mornings, Burgh castle appears exactly as it was when it was first built – including ramparts, bastions and flying banners.

And on 3 July there's said to be a ghost that nobody can explain: a figure wrapped in a white flag that's thrown from the ruins to the foreshore.

Caister Castle

Caister Castle is the remains of a late medieval and Tudor fortified and moated manor house. It lies just off Castle Road in West Caister – OS map reference TG 5044 1226. It's open to the public as part of the car museum.

The beginnings of the castle

The house was built for Sir John Fastolf on the site of an earlier fortified manor house, around 1432; it took 30 years to build, with the last parts being roofed and tiled in 1468. It was the first castle in England to be built of brick, and more than 1.7 million bricks were delivered or made on the site (although some were used for Hellesdon House, one of Fastolf's other properties in the county). The six-storeyed solar tower which still remains in the north-west corner of the original quadrangle stands at a stunning 98 feet tall. Apart from the curtain wall, towers and a water gate, the castle fell into ruins around 1600 after a new house was built nearby. At one point, the castle moat was connected to a creek and it was possible to sail out to sea from the castle.

Caister Castle.

Tradition says that Fastolf used part of the money he got for ransoming John II (the King of France) at the Battle of Verneuil in 1429 to pay for the castle. Earlier in the year Fastolf had won the Battle of Herrings at Rouvray while bringing supplies from Paris for the siege; the battle got its name because Fastolf used barrels of fish as a stockade.

Sir John Fastolf

Fastolf has been identified wrongly with Shakespeare's Falstaff – who was originally called Sir John Oldcastle, but Elizabeth I ordered Shakespeare to rename his

Caister Castle, view from interior.

character to avoid offending the Oldcastle family. The real Sir John Fastolf, unlike the Shakespearean character, was very far from being a coward: he fought at Agincourt, was at the sieges of Caen and Rouen, and was the lieutenant of Normandy in 1422. He was made a knight-banneret in 1424 and a knight of the garter in 1426. After his victory at the Battle of Herrings in 1429 he was forced to retreat, and Lord Talbot – who was captured during the retreat – accused him of being a coward and wanted him removed from the Order of the Garter. However, during a very lengthy case (it was still being heard in the 1440s), Fastolf was vindicated. His contemporary Sir Thomas Wriothesly called him 'a great builder, having built Caistor Hall in Norfolk, a royal palace in Southwark, and a special good master to the officers of arms'.

Fastolf returned to England from France in 1439, but because he was linked to opponents of the government he spent the next 20 years being persecuted – firstly by the Duke of Suffolk, who raided Fastolf's lands, and then by Somerset who nearly had him arraigned for treason. Fastolf managed to hang on to his money, but the experience made him bitter.

The siege of Caister

Fastolf wanted to build a college of priests at Caister Castle, but he'd had to spend so much time at law defending himself and his property that he hadn't been able to set up the college. However, he'd become friendly with his neighbour John Paston, and towards the end of his life redrafted his will to give Paston all his properties – the idea being that Paston would set up the college. Fastolf died on 5

November 1458 after 'an hectic fever and asthma' lasting 148 days and was buried in St Benet's Abbey; his funeral, costing £600 (equivalent to over £300,000 in terms of today's money), was incredibly lavish.

But the trouble started when his heirs, Yelverton and Howes, refused to accept the fact that Fastolf had left the castle to John Paston. To safeguard the castle, Margaret Paston had to move there; she she wasn't happy, because it was draughtier than their house at Oxnead and not as comfortable. She complained to her son, John the Elder. Eventually, John persuaded his younger brother (also named John) to move in so their mother could return to Oxnead.

Meanwhile, Yelverton and Howes sold their rights to the Duke of Norfolk – who decided that he wanted Caister Castle. John Paston the Younger had once been the Duke of Norfolk's servant, so it upset the duke even more because he hated the idea of one of his servants owning something that he thought ought to be his. In 1469, when the Earl of Warwick rebelled and imprisoned the king, the Duke of Norfolk saw his chance to act and besieged the castle with 3,000 men. Inside the castle, there were about thirty men, including John the Younger, four professional soldiers that John the Elder had hired eight months earlier, and Thomas Stumps – who apparently had no hands but still believed he could shoot a crossbow.

The Duke of Norfolk added insult to injury by offering a peace settlement ten days into the siege: if the Pastons gave up the castle, he would pay compensation for any wrongs done to the Pastons… *if* the courts found in their favour. Considering that nobody would stand up to the Duke of Norfolk except the king, who was otherwise occupied, this was hardly a settlement!

Margaret Paston was furious with her son John the Elder for not helping at Caister. She wrote to him saying that his brother 'and his fellowship stand in great jeopardy', various people were dead or badly hurt and 'gunpowder and arrows are lacking'. The castle was 'badly broken by Duke of Norfolk's guns' and she thought that without help John the Younger and his people were likely to die and the castle would be razed to the ground. John the Elder wrote back three days later, pointing out that the people she named 'were alive and merry' the previous Saturday and he doubted anyone would have come out alive to tell her they were dead (he was very brave to answer his mother back, considering just what a strong woman Margaret Paston was!). He said that he had agreed a truce, which he thought would be extended for a week, and he hoped the situation would be resolved. Margaret wrote back saying that she wasn't telling stories, she'd been given information and she would continue to report to him – in other words, if he didn't do something she would nag him intolerably.

The castle was forced to yield to the Duke of Norfolk, and John the Younger wrote to his brother saying that he owed the men thanks for what they did, and they only surrendered because 'we were sore lacking in victuals, gunpowder and men's hearts, and lack of certainty of rescue drove us to the treaty'.

During the siege, two of the Duke of Norfolk's men had been shot and killed. Despite the fact that the men were only shot because they had been besieging the castle, the duke accused the Pastons and their retainers of murder. The trial took place at the assizes at Norwich, the following year. Although the matter was eventually dropped, according to the nineteenth-century historian Dawson Turner, the Duke of Norfolk bribed the widows with 100 shillings each to continue the prosecution.

The enmity between the Pastons and the Duke of Norfolk went deep, particularly as the Duke of Norfolk didn't even live at Caister Castle, once he had possession: he simply shut it up, with three men to keep guard. The duke's men also stole sheep from the Pastons at Mautby, and took potshots at their tenant farmers.

John the Elder took the Duke of Norfolk to court, in an attempt to get the castle back. The Pastons also fought against him, on the side of Henry VI, at the Battle of Barnet in 1471.

When the Duke of Norfolk died in January 1476, John the Elder was quick to reoccupy the castle. John the Younger advised him to get a patent from the king sealed as soon as possible, before the Duke of Norfolk's widow complained and persuaded the king to give the castle back to her. John managed to get the patent from the king in July 1476, but didn't enjoy Caister for long – he died from the plague in London in 1479.

End of the castle

The Pastons left Caister Castle in 1599 for their house at Oxnead, and the castle gradually fell into ruins. In 1659, it was sold to a London moneylender; and it stopped being lived in during the mid-nineteenth century. Nowadays the ruins are part of a museum which houses the UK's largest private collection of cars.

Spooks

Caister Castle allegedly has a spectral horse-drawn hearse, driven by a headless horseman. He circles the courtyard seven times – and seeing the ghost is a warning of an impending death in the family.

Castle Acre

Castle Acre is a rarity: it's the remains of a Norman planned settlement, including a castle, the town, a parish church and the monastery. (Ordnance Survey map references: for the castle, TF 8182 1505; for the bailey gate, TF 819 152; and for the priory, TF 814 148.) According to Pevsner, E.S. Armitage called it 'perhaps the finest castle earthworks in England'. The castle and the priory are both open to the public.

The castle

The castle is an eleventh-century stone fortified manor house, with twelfth-century stone ringwork and a bailey castle. The bailey gate is thirteenth-century, and there were originally two of them; the main road into the village runs between the twin towers.

There were two storeys; the ground floor was used for storage and the upper floor had living accommodation with an external staircase. According to Pevsner, Castle Acre is unusual because the earliest stone building in the centre of the upper ward was a domestic building rather than a military one.

Castle Acre Castle.

Strategically, the castle was positioned on two major communication routes: the river Nar (running east-west) and Peddars Way, a Roman road running north-south on the west side of East Anglia.

On the site there was already a hall belonging to a Saxon thane called Toki, who had substantial landholdings in Norfolk, Suffolk and Cambridgeshire. The hall was replaced by a castle (really a manor house) built by William de Warenne after the Norman conquest; this castle was replaced by a keep in the twelfth century. The site became derelict in the fourteenth century.

Beginnings of the castle

Work on the castle began in the 1070s by William de Warenne, who had fought with William the Conqueror at Hastings and was one of the four men left in

Castle Acre Castle, plate from Thomas Kitson Cromwell's Excursions Through Norfolk, Vol II, *1819.*

charge of England when William I returned to Normandy in 1067. De Warenne also had to deal with the rebellion of Ralph de Gael in Norwich (see page 98). He was the largest landowner in Norfolk, and frequently tried to enlarge his estates by asserting his lordship over freemen who weren't actually assigned to him. However, he managed his estates well, and tripled the size of his sheep flock at Castle Acre.

De Warenne had been created the Earl of Surrey in early 1088 for standing by William Rufus after William the Conqueror's death. When England was invaded, de Warenne fought for the king – but he was wounded by an arrow at the siege of Pevensey Castle and died in June 1088. A few years previously, he'd gone on a pilgrimage to Rome, but had been forced to stop at Cluny because of the war in Italy. His experiences at Cluny made him decide to establish a Cluniac priory in England – which he did, at Lewes. He had planned to establish a second Cluniac priory at Castle Acre, but died before he could put his plans into practice. Along with his wife Gundrada (who died in childbirth at Castle Acre in 1085), he was buried at Lewes Priory.

Rebellion, exile… and carrying off a countess

William de Warenne's son, also named William de Warenne, succeeded him and became the second Earl of Surrey. William (II) de Warenne was a hothead who got on badly with Henry I and ridiculed him – and then joined Robert Curthose, the Duke of Normandy, when he invaded England in July 1101. Henry gave the Duke of Normandy an annuity of 3,000 marks (£2,000 – the equivalent of over a million pounds in terms of today's money) to buy him off; but de Warenne lost his estates and was sent into exile. Two years later, the Duke of Normandy went to see Henry I and persuaded him to reinstate de Warenne; in exchange, the Duke of Normandy gave up the annuity. From then on, de Warenne was a staunch supporter of Henry I, and his support of the king in the battle against Louis VI of France in 1119 helped to decide the victory.

De Warenne married Isabel, the widow of Robert, count of Meulan. There were rumours that she'd been 'carried off' by an earl; although the details have been lost to history, it's tempting to speculate that the earl concerned was indeed the Earl of Surrey – particularly as he'd been a hothead in his youth, and he married Isabel very shortly after Count Robert's death in 1118.

He died in 1138, after attending Henry I's deathbed in 1135, being appointed the Governor of Rouen and the Pays de Caux, and supporting King Stephen's charters.

From manor house to fortress

William (II) de Warenne's son – also called William – succeeded him in 1138. During the reign of Stephen and Matilda, the country was in a state of civil unrest; Earl Warenne (as he called himself) rebuilt the castle at Castle Acre in 1140. He gutted the house and doubled the thickness of the walls, deepened the ditch and replaced the wooden palisade with a flint wall and crenellated parapet. He supported Stephen and Matilda, but in 1147 he decided to join the second Crusade and put his brother Reginald in charge. He was killed in Laodicea in January 1148.

End of the castle

John de Warenne (born c. 1231) was originally a supporter of Simon de Montfort, but deserted the cause due to his friendship with Prince Edward. He fought alongside Henry III at the Battle of Lewes in 1264, and fled abroad when the king was defeated. His estates were confiscated by de Montfort's supporters, but John returned to fight with Edward at the Battle of Evesham and was formally pardoned and his estates returned in 1268. He continued to work for Edward in military campaigns and diplomacy, and died in 1304.

He was succeeded by his grandson, John de Warenne, who changed sides several times in the fight between Edward II and Isabella (see Castle Rising, page 38) but remained loyal to their son, Edward III. John's marriage was unhappy and he was excommunicated in 1316 for adultery; he had several children by his mistress, Matilda de Nerford. In 1316 he gave Castle Acre Castle to Aymer de Valence, Earl of Pembroke (who helped him in his suit for divorce), but the castle eventually came to Richard, the Earl of Arundel, in 1374. Richard had little interest in maintaining the castle and it probably became derelict around this time. After Richard's execution for treason in 1397, the castle was given to the

Duke of Norfolk, but a survey gave its value as 'nil'. The lands became used for agriculture and the stone of the castle was used as building material in the village. The castle was sold to Sir Thomas Gresham, and then to Sir Thomas Cecil. In 1615 the property was sold to Sir Edward Coke for £8,000 (the equivalent of over a million pounds in terms of today's money). It's said that James I was concerned about how large Coke's estates were becoming, but Coke assured him he was only acquiring 'an Acre' (i.e. the whole of Castle Acre!). That year, Coke made some repairs to the battlements in what's thought to be the one of the earliest attempts as conservation of a ruin.

English Heritage has looked after the site since 1984.

Beginnings of the priory

William (II) de Warenne was the one who founded the priory, in accordance with his father's wishes, in the eleventh century. The ruins are extensive, including a sixteenth-century two-storey stone porch for the prior's lodging.

The original church was built within the area of the castle, but it turned out to be too small. William (II) de Warenne granted the 25 to 30 monks a charter and land, and also let them use his stonemason Ulmar to work on the building. Building work on the priory started some time around 1090 – there are letters from Herbert de Losinga, the Bishop of Norwich, which refer to the building of the priory. It was home to a community of 26 monks until its dissolution on 22 November 1537, when the king granted the property to Thomas Howard, the Duke of Norfolk.

In 1929 his descendant, the Earl of Leicester, appointed the Commissioners of HM Works (now English Heritage) its guardians under the terms of the Ancient Monuments Act 1913.

Castle Acre Priory.

Castle Acre Priory – view from Henry Harrod's Castles and Convents of Norfolk, *1857.*

Scandals, sieges...

In 1259, the Prior of Lewes was ordered to punish the Prior of Castle Acre for not coming to the yearly chapter at Cluny, despite a formal summons. The prior had also pledged the seal of the convent on behalf of people outside the monastery, which was forbidden.

In May 1283, William of Shoreham, the prior of Castle Acre, fortified the monastery against the Prior of Lewes so he couldn't be thrown out in favour of Benedict of Cluny. The Earl of Warenne's men helped him, and the Abbot of Cluny wrote to the Earl of Warenne, telling him to allow the new prior into the monastery. Benedict of Cluny finally got possession, the following year.

In 1293, the priory was in trouble again; it was in debt for 1,000 marks (i.e. £666 13s 4d – equivalent to nearly £275,000 in terms of today's money).

And in 1351 the king told the serjeant-at-arms to arrest the monks of Castle Acre, who had 'spurned the habit of their order and were vagabonds in England in secular habit'.

.... and spooks

The priory used as setting for a film of Edgar Allen Poe's ghost story 'The Tomb of Ligeia' in 1964. Allegedly, there are two ghostly monks in Swaffham who try make their way back to Castle Acre Priory, but never quite get there!

Dissolution

Legh and Ap Rice visited the monastery in 1536 and their comperta claimed that seven of the monks had confessed to 'foul sins'. However, it's unlikely, because the Bishop of Norwich considered the prior, Thomas Malling, as a candidate for the suffragan bishopric of Thetford, and also the king appointed Malling as a justice in the county.

The priory was dissolved in November 1537 and the site was granted to the Duke of Norfolk.

Castle Rising Castle

Castle Rising Castle is the remains of a Norman keep with a fourteenth-century brick curtain wall. It lies just off Lynn Road in Castle Rising, not far from the A149 (OS map reference TF 6660 2457) and is in the care of English Heritage. It is open to the public.

The beginnings of the castle

The keep was begun in 1138 by William d'Albini (see New Buckenham on page 86) for his new wife Adelize, the widow of Henry I. The stone came from Barnack in Northamptonshire, and was whitewashed. The original buildings included an eleventh-century Norman church (the foundations of which still remain); the earthworks, dating from the same time as the keep, cover an area of twelve acres. The site itself was originally four miles nearer to the sea than it is now.

According to Pevsner, the keep was based on the plan of Norwich castle, so it's a hall keep rather than a tower keep, and it's one of the largest and most decorated keeps in England. The building remained unfinished until the thirteenth century, when the earthworks were increased in height by five metres.

The castle had a deer park and a rabbit warren (at that point, rabbits were a luxury food – see Thetford Warren Lodge, page 135), but wasn't lived in after the middle of the sixteenth century. In

Castle Rising Castle.

about 1588, it was reported that Stephen Bull, the warrener, had bred so many rabbits that their digging had affected the castle; the banks and walls were 'decayed' and the place was in danger of falling down. Luckily, however, it was thought that the materials were practically worthless, so the castle wasn't demolished: it was simply left to decay.

Castle Rising Castle.

The siege of 1312

According to the nineteenth-century historian Henry Harrod, Robert de Montalt – who lived at Castle Rising in the early fourteenth century – took the prior, mayor and commonalty of Lynn to court. He claimed that while he'd been in King's Lynn on business, when the King was abroad, he'd been assaulted and captured. Nicholas de Northampton and his friends insulted Robert and his men, unfurled their banners 'in a warlike manner' and chased them to de Montalt's house in the town. They besieged it, broke down the doors and beat up de Montalt and his men. They also stole arms, swords, spurs, money and jewels worth £40 (the equivalent of nearly £16,000 in today's money), then threw his men into prison and imprisoned de Montalt in the house of Robert Costin for two days. They forced him to stop all legal actions against the mayor and commonalty, and give them the right to appoint a bailiff to collect his profits from the toll and port. Then they carried him to the market place and made him say it in public, as well as swearing a bond of £2,000 that he wouldn't go back on his word – and then 'committed divers other enormities' to the damage of £2,000 and also 100,000 marks to him personally (a little under £67,000, or an incredible £26 million in today's money).

The mayor and commonalty said they hadn't committed a breach of the peace, but de Montalt had – his men had wounded two of the town's burgesses to the point where 'their lives were despaired of', and refused to be dealt with by the law. De Montalt came to their aid 'with force and arms' and took them to his house; the mayor and his men followed and captured them so they could bring them to justice. The mayor also claimed that de Montalt had given the deeds of grant of his own accord and hadn't been forced to sign them.

The judgement went in favour of de Montalt, and the mayor had to tax the town very heavily to raise the £6,000 (equivalent to almost two and a half million pounds in today's money) he was forced to give de Montalt in damages.

Scandals and spooks: the She-Wolf of France

The most famous – or perhaps infamous – person to live at Castle Rising was Queen Isabella, the widow and alleged murderess of Edward II. She lived in a private suite to the south of the keep from her arrest in 1331 until 1358. Although some sources claim she was a prisoner who was shut up in the castle, the supervision was extremely light and she was able to go into Lynn, Norwich and Windsor; her surroundings were comfortable rather than austere.

Isabella's marriage to Edward II had been unhappy. Before the coronation on 25 February 1308, Edward had already sent her father's wedding gifts to his favourite, Piers Gaveston. She complained to her uncle that Gaveston usurped her place and her husband kept her short of funds. The funding issue wasn't strictly true, but Edward wasn't a popular king; he listened too much to his favourites (firstly Gaveston and then the Despensers), broke his promises of reforms and was deeply in debt.

The barons rebelled and Edward was forced to sign ordinances in 1311 to stop him spending more money without parliamentary approval or siphoning off funds – and to dismiss the 'evil counsellors' (i.e Gaveston); although he gave the order to publish the ordinances, the very next day he started to persuade the pope to annual the ordinances.

The next ten years were spent in political instability; although Isabella did her best to mediate between Edward and the barons she wasn't successful. Edward continued to mismanage the realm, losing disastrous battles against the Scots. Civil war broke out in 1321; Edward won in 1322 and had the ordinances overturned once and for all. He executed those who had acted against him and confiscated their land. But he was still heavily influenced by the Despensers; by 1325 Isabella realised that the only way of regaining her influence and her wealth (her lands had been seized in 1324) was to have her son crowned as king.

Anglo-French relations deteriorated again and Edward sent Isabella to negotiate with her brother, Charles IV of France. She did so, but stayed in Paris even after Edward ordered her home, saying that she wouldn't return until the Despensers were removed from court. Charles supported her refusal to return, claiming that Edward had expelled her from England and wanted her dead. She ended up spending time with Englishmen exiled as traitors, and fell in love with Roger Mortimer.

Edward was furious and was rumoured to keep a knife in his hose to kill her – and said that if he had no other weapon he would crush her with his feeth.

In 1326 Isabella invaded England with Mortimer as her captain, saying that she wanted to end Edward's misgovernment. The country supported her, and

Edward fled to Wales with the Despensers. Isabella proclaimed her son guardian of the realm; the Despensers were captured and executed, and Edward was captured and taken to Kenilworth. Parliament was summoned in 1327 and a list of six articles was presented to the assembly, showing why Edward should no longer reign. He resigned the throne and Edward III was crowned.

There were several plots to rescue Edward II; after the third conspiracy was discovered, it was announced that he had died at Berkeley Castle. It's possible that his death was due to natural causes; it's widely believed that he was murdered on the orders of Mortimer and Isabella. There was also a rumour that he'd escaped (and later his half-brother was executed for plotting to restore Edward II).

Meanwhile, Isabella and Mortimer governed the country; they took the Despensers' lands and much of the royal demesne. They also negotiated peace with France and with Scotland, recognising the independence of Scotland – and also keeping the £20,000 that Robert I paid in reparation for the damage done by his troops in northern England. Anyone who opposed them was implicated in false plots, executed and their lands taken. Mortimer interrogated the king about his loyalty, and eventually Edward III had them both arrested in Nottingham. He had Mortimer executed as a traitor.

Although Isabella was initially under guard, she moved to Castle Rising and received Edward III regally on his visits. Far from being shut up, she was allowed to travel to Northampton, Walsingham and Langley; she also celebrated Edward III's birthday with him at Norwich in 1344 – the feast apparently included an 'enormous pie, wondrously large'. He gave her £3,000 a year for her expenses, so she didn't live in penury (£3,000 in 1344 was equivalent to over a million pounds in terms of today's money).

She died at Hertford Castle on 23 August 1358; despite evidence from her own household book placing her at Hertford, it's often claimed that Isabella died at Castle Rising and her spirit haunts the place. Some of the legends claim that she went mad towards the end of her life and roamed the battlements late at night; her screams and mad laughter have been heard on stormy nights, or on nights with a full moon.

The tunnels of Castle Rising

There is a legend that a tunnel ran from Castle Rising to the Red Mount in King's Lynn – this is partly linked to the claim that Isabella was imprisoned at Castle Rising and used the tunnel to travel undetected by her son. As she was allowed to travel, it's unlikely that the tunnel existed.

Entrances to tunnels were discovered at both places; however, when they were excavated, it was discovered that the King's Lynn tunnel was extremely short and the Castle Rising tunnel was actually just another entrance to an inner stairway.

*Village sign at East Rudham commemorating the
priory at Coxford.*

Coxford Priory

Coxford Priory is the remains of an Augustinian abbey at East Rudham; only the north transept arch is still standing, along with masonry from the walls of the chancel and transept. It lies just off the road to Broomsthorpe (OS map reference TF 844 290) and is on private land. It is not open to the public.

The beginnings of the priory

William Cheney founded a priory in the church of St Mary in East Rudham in the mid 1200s. In 1215 the priory was moved to the eastern boundary of the parish of Coxford; around ten canons and the abbot lived there, and it was one of the wealthiest Augustinian houses in Norfolk. There may well be Roman remains nearby, as a hoard of Roman coins was found on the site in the eighteenth century.

Remains of the priory at Coxford.

Scandals: coursing, chess and chatting up girls

Archbishop Peckham visited the priory in January 1281, and was so shocked by the lack of discipline among the monks that he sent the prior a long letter outlining his faults. The archbishop said that the prior was lacking in religious zeal, didn't attend divine service regularly and failed to control his subordinates. This negligence meant that the canons went out coursing with hounds (possibly poaching), attending banquets and chatting with girls; the archbishop added that the priory was a scandal and a joke in the whole neighbourhood.

His solution was to appoint two monks to act with the prior in controlling the monks, and to set up a list of rules. Firstly, any monks who wanted to follow the horses could only do so on foot, not on horseback – and could only go hunting if the prior was there with them. Any 'incontinent' (i.e. unchaste) monks were not allowed out unless it was 'very necessary' and they had others 'of good fame' with them – if they left anyway, they would be expelled for five days from the order and would have to take their meals sitting on the ground. If they spoke to women they would be punished unless they could produce witnesses of their innocence – and chatterboxes would also be punished. Chess and other games were forbidden, and Robert de Hunstanton was named as the worst offender as he'd been the one to teach the others chess.

Any monk who fell foul of the rules would be put on bread and water – one day for a first breach, two days if they were still refractory, and the punishment would fit the crime so 'as his insolence, so his fast'.

Two hundred years later, things still weren't good at; at the visitation of 1492, Bishop Nix noted that the hospital wasn't open to the infirm, the novices needed a grammar master, the refectory was too cold to eat in and there was 'no honest recreation provided' for the canons.

At a further visitation in 1514, the prior, John Matthew, admitted that morning prayers weren't celebrated, the other monks were disobedient and quarrelsome, and John Berdon had 'taken to flight' three or four times so was currently in prison. (In other words, he'd run away – and the penance for apostasy, i.e. leaving a religious institution without permission or a licence, tended to be excommunication and imprisonment.) Bishop Nix had to apply injunctions: firstly to make the monks observe silence, secondly to make them provide suitable food for the sick, and thirdly about the obedience and religious behaviour of the canons 'in the quire'. All was apparently well in 1520 – though it's possible that much was swept under the carpet, because the same problems as the 1514 visitation were mentioned in the visitation of 1532. Henry Salter, the prior, admitted that Robert Porter was guilty of 'incontinence' (i.e. he'd been unchaste) but had been corrected, and also that he hadn't done his accounts.

Legh and Ap Rice visited in 1536 and claimed, as usual, that the monks were 'incontinent' (in other words, they didn't keep their vow of celibacy). They named in particular the subprior, William Neville, who was one of the oldest canons there! However, the king's commissioners visited later that year and reported the monks were 'alle Prystes of goode name'.

Dissolution

The priory was dissolved in 1536 and the property was sold off in January 1537 – including the table at the high altar, an alabaster table in the quire, the organ and the 'stuff in the churche' (the latter for 7 shillings and 8 pence). The site and possessions were granted to Thomas, Duke of Norfolk, and the sarcophagus of a previous friar was removed to the church at Houghton.

Sarcophagus of former prior of Coxford at Houghton Church.

The priory was partly demolished by Sir Roger Townshend, who used the stone to build Raynham Hall in 1619.

Spooks: the ghost of Raynham Hall

Although Raynham Hall is built from the materials of the priory, its ghost has nothing to do with the priory. She's a lady in a brown brocade dress, with sunken eyes and hollow cheeks, and it's thought that she's the ghost of Lady Dorothy Walpole.

So the story goes, Lady Dorothy fell in love with Charles, the second Viscount Townshend, but her father refused to let them marry; she ended up having an affair with Lord Wharton, a well-known rake. When Wharton left the country, Dorothy's father married her off to Viscount Townshend (better known as 'Turnip' Townshend, the agriculturalist). Years later, Townshend found out about his wife's past; he ordered her to be locked in her rooms and have no further contact with their children. Lady Dorothy allegedly threw herself down the stairs and died (though records show that she died from smallpox) and she supposedly haunts the stairs.

The novelist Captain Marryat saw a woman carrying a lamp while he was visiting the hall in 1836. When she drew nearer, he realised that he'd seen her before – she was the subject of the portrait of the 'Brown Lady', which hung in his room. She looked at him in a 'diabolical manner' and he shot at her – though the bullet went straight through her and hit the door behind her. In 1849, another guest, Major Loftus, saw a lady in an old-fashioned dress who disappeared as he looked at her.

During a photo shoot at the hall in September 1936, photographers Captain Provand and Indre Shira from *Country Life* magazine saw a misty form on the stairs and took the photograph. The image of a hooded figure was developed in front of an independent witness, chemist Benjamin Jones, and experts at the time said that there was no sign of tampering with the film.

However, according to researcher and barrister Alan Murdie, it's possible that the film had a double exposure or the image was caused by a fault in the camera – and Provand admitted later that the camera had a problem with the bellows and he was worried about light getting in. So did they photograph a ghost... or was it just a simple trick of the light?

Crabhouse Nunnery, Wiggenhall St Mary Magdalen

Nothing now remains of the twelfth-century Augustine nunnery of Crabhouse, apart from the name 'The Priory' of the house built in its former place, and the name 'Crabbe Abbey' of a nearby farmhouse.

Beginnings of the Nunnery

The nunnery was started by Lena, the daughter of Godric de Lynne, who wanted to find a desert place where she could pray without being disturbed. She found a place near the banks of the River Ouse: Crabhouse, in the parish of Wiggenhall – far away from any human habitation, in the middle of marshland – and started to build a small wooden shack as a chapel. According to the nineteenth-century scholar Augustus Jessopp, the original church was a 'wretched little shanty' built from driftwood and thatched with reeds; gradually, she tamed the land and made a farm. But when the Domesday commissioners arrived, they wanted to know who'd given them the land; when Lena explained that she and her nuns had reclaimed the land, the commissioner didn't believe her. In the end, she had to lie and say a local landowner had given her the property, and he duly gave her a charter.

Who the landowner was isn't stated, but the dates we do have are rather later: the site was granted to the nuns by Roger, the prior of Reynham, in 1181 and the nunnery was dedicated to St John the Evangelist, Mary Magdalen, Thomas and Peter.

The original site was wrecked by a huge flood, and only one nun decided to stay: Joan, who built a cabin in the cemetery of the church of St Mary Magdalen in Wiggenhall, and became a hermit. The other nuns made a new site, early in the thirteenth century.

According to Jessopp, the land reverted to the lord of the manor, Allan FitzRichard, who gave it to his sister and her husband Aylmer Kok (the chaplain of Crabhouse), and they built the new chapel; gradually people started to ask if they could become a nun there, and brought lands and endowments with them. By the fourteenth century, it had become a fashionable convent (much of their documents are written in French rather than Latin!), and many of the nuns were daughters of wealthy landowners. One in particular, John de Ingoldesthorpe, gave the nuns a great deal of land and money for his daughter's dowry.

So dear and worth so little

Agnes de Methelwold was the prioress from 1315 until her death in 1344. She spent over £100 in silver (the equivalent of over £40,000 in terms of today's money) to build a hall, a stable, a bakery and a noble room, and she was clearly a good administrator as she assigned various rents to pay for particular items for the house. Some provided the food (bread, ale, flesh, fish and red herring); some for repairs; others for clothing and linen. Her accounts also mention the repair of sea and marsh dykes, the wages of household servants, cattle fodder, and fuel.

However, she made one big mistake which haunted her. Farmer Aleyn Brid offered her his lands in exchange for an annuity (a pension for the rest of his life) and a downpayment. Agnes, seeing how old Aleyn and his wife were, thought that she was getting a bargain, but it turned out to be very far from it. Aleyn and his wife lived on for years and years, and the land turned out to be barren and worthless. *'Si cher terre de cy petit value unkes ne fut achate!'* said Agnes – i.e. land so dear and worth so little never was bought...

The amazing Joan

Joan Wiggenhall is one of the real characters of the nunnery. She was elected prioress in 1420 and embarked on a huge building programme – probably too huge, as it left the house in debt, but her energy and drive were still absolutely amazing.

She started by taking down the barn by the gatehouse in October 1420 – and she'd rebuilt it before the next harvest, at a cost of £45, 9 shillings and 6 pence (the equivalent of almost £20,000 in terms of modern money) in addition to the cost of timber from their own lands and the tiles reused from the old barn. However, she didn't pay all of it from convent funds – she persuaded their patron, John de Ingoldesthorpe, to give them money towards it. The following year, she extended the prioress's lodgings and rebuilt the convent's part of the chancel in St Peter's at Wiggenhall. The year after, she worked on the precinct walls and the cloister; and the year after that, her attention turned to the convent's church, which was in very poor condition. On advice, she took it down and rebuilt it, 'Trostynge to the helpe of oure Lorde and to the grete charite of goode cristen men.' She did indeed get charitable assistance, from her cousin Edmund Perys, the rector of Crabhouse. Among other donations, he gave her two antiphonaries rumoured to be worth 20 marks each (the equivalent of nearly £6,000 in terms of today's money).

She died in 1445, just after her building work was completed.

Marriage in the monastery

Unusually, on 9 September 1476, a marriage was celebrated at the nunnery; the bishop of Norwich gave Thomas Hunston and Margaret Keroyle a special licence to be married there. Instead of giving the vicar of St Mary Magdalen his usual fee, they gave him a composition!

Scandals

In 1514, at the visitation, prioress Elizabeth Bredon (who'd been prioress for 24 years at this point) said that all the sisters were obedient except one, Mary Stutfield; the house was in debt for 10 marks (£6 8s – the equivalent of nearly £3,000 in today's money) but their debtors also owed them 5 marks.

However, the nuns told a different story. They said that Elizabeth's discipline was lax and she was tactless; the juniors in turn were really saucy to their seniors and picked quarrels with the others. The nuns didn't confess frequently enough; the roof of the Lady Chapel needed repair, and the prioress didn't keep any accounts. But the one huge scandal was that of Agnes Smyth: she'd been seduced by Simon Prentis, a local wealthy landowner, and had a child by him. Agnes confessed to her sins, and the child had died.

The bishop insisted that the sisters should obey the prioress, and Agnes had to take the 'lowest seat' for a month. She also had to say the whole psalter seven times within that month.

Six years later, Margaret Studefeld (Mary's sister) was the prioress and the report was 'omnia bene'. However, the scandal of Agnes had been too much for the convent – respectable landowners didn't want their daughters' names tarnished, and as a result they didn't send novices along to the nunnery with new endowments. The nunnery became poor, and at the end there were only four people left.

Dissolution

John Ap Rice and Thomas Legh made their usual scandalous comperta in 1536, and used the story of Agnes to claim that the prioress and the three remaining nuns had all been unchaste. According to them, the prioress had had a baby; two of the other nuns had had children by single men, and the other nun had had two children – one fathered by a priest and one by a layman. The king's commissioners reported differently; they said 'ther name is goode', and wrote about the prioress 'Bona fama et conversatio'.

The nunnery was dissolved in 1537 and all the goods were sold to Henry Webbe in February 1537 for £9 (except the plate, kept by Richard Southwell for the king, valued at £5 15s).

Creake Abbey

Creake Abbey is the remains of an Augustinian abbey at North Creake. It lies off the Burnham Road (OS map reference TF 8552 3952). It's in the care of English Heritage and is open to the public.

The beginnings of the abbey

Sir Robert de Nerford, the governor of Dover Castle, had founded a hospital in North Creake dedicated to St Bartholomew, the patron saint of tanners. His widow, Alice, turned it into a priory dedicated to the Blessed Virgin in 1206; there was a master, William Geyst, four chaplains and 13 poor brethren. The chapel was consecrated in 1221; ten years later, Henry III sanctioned the change to the

Creake Abbey.

status of an abbey and gave them the right to elect their own prior. The master became the prior and the chaplains became Augustinian canons.

Disastrous fire

In 1378, the church and buildings burned down. The church was rebuilt and Richard II, as patron, gave them £46 13s and 4d towards the cost.

The end of the priory

In 1506, plague hit the abbey and killed all the canons within a week. Giles Shevington, the abbot, was the last survivor and died on 12 December 1506. Because there were no canons left to elect a successor, the house was dissolved and returned to the crown. The abbey was given to Lady Margaret Beaufort (Henry VII's mother) and she settled the land and revenues on Christ's College, Cambridge.

Spooks, sorcery and treasure-hunting

There were rumours of treasure being buried at the abbey to stop Henry VIII's assessors getting it – and in 1528, William Stapleton, a monk from St Benet's Abbey (see page 62) decided to try and find it.

Stapleton had been a complete failure as a monk. He never got up in time for Matins, and was always being punished for not doing his duty in church; unsurprisingly, he wanted to buy a dispensation so he could leave the monastic life behind. He spent his time studying how to find treasure by 'scrying'; while he was still at St Benet's, Denys of Hofton brought him two books, *Thesaurus Spirituum* and *Secreta Secretorum*, as well as a little ring, a plate, a circle, and also a 'sword for the art of digging' (i.e. finding treasure in ancient barrows and the like). Stapleton then negotiated a dispensation for six months, by the end of which he'd planned to raise enough money from treasure-hunting to buy a full dispensation.

Denys of Hofton agreed to put Stapleton in touch with two men who had placards (i.e. a licence to dig up treasure) and offered to help him in exchange for a share of the spoils. Stapleton found nothing at Norwich, Sidestrand or Felmingham, and was panicking about not being able to buy his dispensation; but he borrowed the money from Richard Thony and some friends, on the understanding that he would go back to 'digging' as soon as he had his dispensation. He warned them that he needed better books in order to do it, and they told him about a man called Leech who claimed to have a book to which the parson of Lessingham had bound a spirit called Andrew Malchus. The parson had apparently called up two other spirits – including one called Oberion, who refused to speak to him. The parson asked Andrew Malchus for an explanation, and discovered it was because Oberion was bound to 'my Lord Cardinal' (i.e. Wolsey).

Stapleton went back to Norwich 'for a season', according to his confession, then went to meet Lord Leonard Marquess at Walsingham. Lord Leonard said he'd heard that Stapleton was skilled at 'digging', and he would make Stapleton his chaplain if he could prove his skill. As a trial, Lord Leonard asked a servant to hide some money in the garden so Stapleton could 'scry' for it – but Stapleton failed to find the hidden treasure.

Next, Stapleton met Sir Robert Porter and the necromancer John Sharpe and headed for Creake Abbey, expecting to find hidden treasure there. Sharpe allegedly called to the spirit of the treasure – but they found nothing. They ended up in London, and then Lord Leonard offered to make him a parish priest. Stapleton accepted, but carried on trying to find treasure. When he still didn't find treasure he went off to London again – and Lord Leonard had him arrested for leaving without a licence. Lord Leonard eventually relented and had Stapleton freed from prison.

And then Mr Wright, a servant of the Duke of Norfolk, talked to Stapleton and told him that his master was 'sore vexed with a spirit by the enchantment of

[Wolsey]'. The Duke of Norfolk didn't get on well with Wolsey (and, years later, in the Tower of London, claimed that Wolsey spent 14 years plotting his destruction), plus in 1521 the Duke of Buckingham, before he was executed for treason, claimed that Wolsey used necromancy to keep the king's favour.

Wright suggested to Stapleton that he might be rewarded if he had the power to remove the spirit, adding that it would also mean favour for Wright and Stapleton's brother if Stapleton could 'feign something, as [he] can do right well, that [he had] done His Grace good in the avoiding of the said spirit'. Even when Stapleton's brother said it would be a good idea, Stapleton was wary, saying he didn't know what to make up.

As Stapleton eventually confessed to Cardinal Wolsey, he was 'blinded with covetize, thinking to have promotion and favour of the said Duke' – so he claimed he'd made a wax image of the duke and had 'sanctified' it. The Duke of Norfolk then wanted to know if Wolsey had a spirit; Stapleton was a little more honest then, and said he didn't know but had heard about the spirit Oberion. The Duke of Norfolk examined him before witnesses, then was clearly either very scared or very superstition and sent Stapleton to Wolsey.

Wolsey's response was to send Stapleton to prison and make him write an account of his behaviour. Stapleton's very long letter to Wolsey ends:

> Whereupon, considering the great folly which hath rested in me, I humbly beseech your Grace to be good and gracious lord unto me, and to take me to your mercy; to the which I wholly refer myself, as I may pray for the preservation of your noble Grace long to endure.

However, at the time, Wolsey's star was on the descendant – he was the scapegoat for Henry VIII's failure to obtain a divorce from Katherine, his foreign policy was failing badly, and in October 1529 he was deprived of office. A year later he was arraigned for treason and died.

As for Stapleton… his fate is obscured by history.

St Withburga's Nunnery and Holy Well, East Dereham

St Withburga's well is in the grounds of the church of St Nicholas on Church Street, East Dereham (OS map reference TF 986 133). The building around the well dates from the fourteenth century but was restored in the nineteenth century. There are no extant remains of the nunnery.

Beginnings of the nunnery

In the early seventh century, Anna was the king of the Angles, and Withburga was his youngest daughter. The story goes that either Withburga founded the nunnery after her father was killed at the battle of Blythburgh in 645, or that her father founded it in 606 and made her the prioress.

The legend of the does

One particular year, the nuns were starving, and Withburga prayed to God to provide for them. After prayers, she fell into a deep sleep and had a vision of the Virgin Mary. Mary told her to send two servants every morning to the bridge; there, they would meet two does, who would allow the servants to milk them and give enough to nourish the nuns.

The next day, she did as she was told, and the servants duly met and milked the does, then turned the milk into butter and cheese. This went on for a while – but the reeve (some sources say the bailiff) became jealous. He set off with his hounds to drive away the deer (some versions of the story have him actually killing the deer with arrows), but his horse stumbled and threw him, and he broke his neck and died.

The legend is commemorated on the town sign at Dereham.

Body-snatching and the miraculous spring

Withburga died in 743 and she was buried in the churchyard until a suitable shrine could be built. The Danes sacked and destroyed the nunnery, and the convent church became the parish church in 798. At the time, her body was discovered uncorrupted, so she was declared a saint and her body was moved within the church.

In about 870, King Edgar suggested that Withburga should be buried at Ely. The townsfolk of Dereham refused flatly. In 984 Brithnoth, the abbot of Ely, and his monks decided on a *'Sanctum Sacrilegium fidele furtum Saintoris rapina'* (i.e. a holy sacrilege or pious fraud – they were going to snatch the body and run). So they held a great feast in Dereham for the townsfolk, making sure they had plenty to eat and even more to drink. When the townsfolk grew sleepy – or were just too drunk to notice – the monks crept in and stole Withburga's body. They had men and carriages ready and waiting on the road, and took the body to Brandon Ferry; from there, they transferred her body to a barge and sailed to Ely. According to the tale in the *Liber Eliensis*, the townsfolk of Dereham caught up with the monks at the river and threw mud at them, but it was too late. The monks of Ely had possession of the body and flatly refused to return it.

When the townsfolk returned to Dereham, they discovered a miracle – a spring had burst forth in the empty tomb, and allegedly it has never run dry since.

In 1752, the spring was arched over and converted into a cold bath; it was repaired in 1793. In 1829, Chambers wrote a report on the town, saying:

> The spring... is very pellucid, and the water very fine; but... is considered too cold for any person to bathe in it whose constitution is net very robust. It is open to the public, and many persons bathe in it during the summer season, and such is the force of habit, that a respectable inhabitant of the town, who died at an advanced age, used this bath daily winter and summer.

In 1880, the bath house was pulled down, but the well – and the stone telling the story of the bodysnatchers – still remains:

The remains of a Tomb which
contained the Remains of
WITHBURGA
youngest Daughter of
ANNAS
King of the East Angles
who died A.D. 684

The Abbot and Monks of Ely stole this precious Relique and translated it to Ely Cathedral where it was interred near her three Royal Sisters A.D. 974

St Withburga's spring, East Dereham.

Gresham Castle

The ruins of Gresham Castle, in the 1950s. Picture courtesy of Norfolk County Council Library and Information Service.

Site of the castle at Gresham.

Village sign at Gresham commemorating the castle.

Gresham Castle is the remains of a fortified manor house on the south side of the village of Gresham, off Chequers Street (OS map reference TG 1666 3807). It's on private land and is not open to the public.

All but the foundations of the castle have disappeared, although the castle was once 130 feet square, with a round tower at each corner. It also had a moat. A sketch of the castle by John Paston, dating from 1471, shows that two of the towers were small, one was large and one was very large.

The beginnings of the castle

Originally the site contained the castle of the De Stuteville family. Sir Edmund Bacon owned the house in 1319, when Edward II granted him a licence to

Site of the castle at Gresham.

crenellate it, and the defences were later strengthened by Thomas Gresham. Geoffrey Chaucer's son Thomas owned the castle at one point – though things are a little confusing here, because it seems that William Paston bought the place in 1427. He bought half of it from Thomas Chaucer, and half of it from Sir William Moleyns, who died the following year.

However, after William died and left the place to his son John, Robert Hungerford (who had married Sir William Moleyns' daughter and taken the title Lord Moleyns) said that he had residual claim to Gresham through his wife. He was encouraged by John Heydon of Baconsthorpe, who didn't get on with the Pastons (see Baconsthorpe Castle on page 6). Moleyns sent men from Wiltshire to seize the castle. John and Margaret Paston weren't in residence at the time and had no idea what was happening, until it was too late and they were unable to defend the castle.

The siege of a thousand men

John Paston started legal proceedings against Lord Moleyns – but Moleyns was friendly with the Duke of Suffolk, Henry VI's chief minister, who was very powerful indeed. It was clear they had an almost impossible fight on their hands.

In April 1448, the Bishop of Winchester offered to help the Pastons. They answered every single one of Moleyns' claims in court, through the medium of sixteen lawyers' meetings; but even when John Paston rode to Salisbury to speak to Moleyns, he got no answer.

In October 1448, Margaret went to Gresham with their two sons (aged 4 and 6 – and both named John, just to make things confusing) and settled in a house right next to the castle. She started collecting rents from their tenant, and discovered that the castle was held by a small group of Moleyns' men, led by John Partridge. She wrote to her husband to him that they'd barred the doors and made 'wickets on every corner of the house' so they could shoot with bows and guns. She asked John to send cross-bows, short poll-axes, and armoured jackets (called 'jacks') – though, touchingly, she was as aware of domestic matters as of military matters, because she also asked him for almonds, sugar and some material to make clothes for the children.

Their friend John Damme spoke to Partridge, and warned the Pastons that he was worried about what Heydon would do. Partridge also said that if the Pastons took the castle, it would be taken back again very quickly.

On 28 January 1449, Moleyns' men arrived to drive Margaret Paston out of Gresham. John Paston sent a petition to the king afterwards, complaining that:

> January last past the seid lord sent to the seid mansion a riotous peple to the nombre of a thowsand persones, with blanket bendes of a sute as riseres a-geyn your pees, arrayd in maner of werre, with curesse, brigaunderes, jakkes, salettes, gleyfes, bowes, arows, pavyse, gonnes, pannys with fier and teynes brenning therein, long cromes to drawe down houses, ladders, pikoys, with which they myned down the walles and long tees with which thei broke up yates and dores.

In other words, they were dressed for war; 1,000 men seems a tad excessive to drive out a woman who was either heavily pregnant or had a new baby at the time, as well as two small children, so it's likely that John was exaggerating. But even so Moleyns' men must have made a frightening spectacle. John described them wearing full armour – the curesse or cuirasse was plate armour, like the 'vest' piece on a traditional suit of armour, with one piece protecting the front and the back. A 'brigaunder' or brigandine was body armour, steel rings or small plates sewn on a jerkin of cloth or leather, and 'jakkes' were short, close-fitting sleeveless jackets, often covered with plates (though the name also referred to a coat of mail). The salet was an open helmet covering the top of the head, often with a tail to protect the back of the neck.

They were carrying weapons of war, too. A gleyfe or glieve was a type of lance, a weapon with a long tapering blade sharpened on one edge and mounted on a long shaft. Bows, arrows and guns ('gonnes') are obvious; the pavys or pavise was a wooden shield made of planks, sometimes covered with linen and painted or lacquered. The pans ('pannys') contained fire and 'teynes' (thin plates of metal) burning; a crome was a crook or hook; pikoys were pikes, a very long thrusting spear with a lance-like head and a body about 9 feet long; a long tee was a type of hook; and 'blanket bends' were long wands, with the bark removed.

Moleyns' men proceeded to break down the walls, then carried Margaret out of the gate. They then went on a rampage, cutting the posts (timber frame) of the house, breaking the rooms and any strongboxes, and taking all the goods and money. Understandably, Margaret fled with the children to the Dammes' house.

John went to Earl of Oxford and told him about the breach of peace. The Earl of Oxford went to Gresham, and Moleyns' men barred the door of the castle against him. Unimpressed, the Earl of Oxford sent a report to the King's Bench.

Moleyns then replaced Partridge with Walter Barrow. Margaret sent a message to Barrow, complaining about the threats she'd received from his men – and, trying a charm offensive, she sent a female servant to deliver the message. Barrow was extremely polite to the servant and said that he wanted to speak to Margaret; he went to see her at the Dammes' house. She spoke to him at the gate and he gave her his word that none of her tenants or servants would be harmed, though she didn't believe him.

In February 1449, Margaret heard a rumour that Moleyns' men were planning to kidnap her and imprison her at Gresham to make John confront them. After months of standing up to the bullies – and, given that she was either pregnant with her daughter Margaret or had a small baby (Margaret's date of birth is unclear but was either 1448 or 1449), she was finally scared away and went to Norwich, where she knew she would be safe.

In September 1450, at last John Paston had the chance to take Moleyns to the court of *oyer* and *terminer* – this was where the justices could sit outside Westminster, hear a case and give judgement. He indicted Moleyns, but the case took absolutely ages. In January 1451, John complained that the castle was 'so decayed' by Molyens' occupation that where it was previously worth 50 marks a year (£32), now it wasn't even worth £20 (the equivalent of under £10,000 in today's money).

Moleyns kept threatening to bring people to Norfolk but didn't. So in February 1451, John Paston took the law into his own hands and recaptured Gresham Castle. Moleyns warned him that he was coming back to take it again, and added that he wouldn't make the tenants pay him the money they'd already paid to the Pastons.

Then the place of the hearing was switched – from Norwich (which had been favourable to the Pastons) to Walsingham (an area heavily under the influence of John Heydon). By the time John reached the hearing, Moleyns had been acquitted of commanding his servants to enter Gresham illegally.

John Paston presented a petition to Parliament and finally won after Moleyn's patron, the Duke of Suffolk, died. However, the castle wasn't fit to live in and remained empty until it crumbled.

Tunnels and treasure

In 1844, the moat was cleaned out; the workers found a drawbridge and an 'entrance to a subterranean passage', though tantalisingly there's no record of whether they followed the passage. It's possible that the passage was actually a drain.

There is a legend about a tunnel running between Gresham Castle and Beeston Priory, and a golden calf is meant to be buried somewhere in the middle of the tunnel (see Beeston Priory, page 12, for further details of the story).

Hempton Priory

Hempton Priory is the remains of an Augustinian priory (OS map reference TF 9165 2886); very little is visible above ground, but Claude Messent places it as 'situated near the mill-dam, a mile south of Fakenham Market Place on the east side of the road to Dereham'. Because it was built at the end of a dam or causeway between Fakenham and Hempton, it was sometimes called Dammesende.

Beginnings of the priory

The priory was originally founded as a hospital by Roger de St Martin in 1135. It became a priory in 1200, dedicated to the honour of St Stephen.

Village sign at Hempton commemorating the priory.

Rows and rebellion

There was a huge row in 1297, when Guy Ferre – who owned the manor of Fakenham – complained to the king that Giles, the prior of Hempton, was grazing his cattle on Guy's land at Pudding Norton. In February 1298, Guy claimed that the prior grabbed his men at Waterden when they were taking goods to the fair at Creake, imprisoned them and stole their goods, as well as 'depasturing' the growing corn in the manor. However, as Giles was still in charge of the priory in 1301, it's likely that Ferre didn't have a just cause and was simply trying his luck to get land from the monastery.

There were further rows in 1299, when villeins in the village of Worstead refused to carry out services on land belonging to the priory in the village. The prior appealed to the sheriff, who sent William de Bedingham in to perfom the legal remedy of distraint (i.e. taking the plough, oxen and implements belonging to the villein until he did the service or paid rent, when the seized possessions would be returned). However, the official was attacked by 66 men and women and was forced to retreat.

Three years later, the prior was allowed to bring the watercourse back to its old bed, running through the court of the priory. However, as economic affairs changed towards the end of the fourteenth century, a row blew up over the watercourse in 1385. The main road to Walsingham led over the millpool 'causey' at Hempton, so it needed to be kept in good repair. The men of Fakenham wanted the road to go through the town instead (so they'd get the custom of pilgrims travelling to the shrine at Walsingham – see page 138) so they kept filing writs to make sure the prior was fined for keeping the water level too high and raising the causey 'beyond customary bounds'. However, if the prior hadn't repaired the causey, he would have been causing peril to the travellers – and that would have led to a fine by the sheriff! So the poor prior couldn't win, whatever he did.

Hunger and silence

At the bishop's visitation of 1514, all was well – but Brother Henry Beteele and Brother Henry Mileham, two of the younger monks, complained that they had nothing to eat until High Mass, except on days when they worked in the fields. Bishop Nix ruled that everyone had to eat at 8am except on fast days, and there had to be one day's silence a week.

The end of the priory

The priory, as one of the smaller foundations, was suppressed in August 1536. Although Richard Southwell, the king's commissioner, gave sums to various people connected with the monastery in January 1537 (including 6s 8d to the 'daye wiff', presumably the cleaner), he gave Prior Henry Salter absolutely nothing. The prior had some debts, including 10s to the butcher for beef, and 12d to the 'butter wyffe'.

Salter isn't mentioned as being a particularly bad character, so it's possible that Southwell was a bit cross because the house didn't have a great deal to leave. The inventory includes items such as 'an old payntyd clothe before ye aulter worne and nothynge worthe' and 'olde cope with a vestment and a decon and subdecon off olde blew sarsnet worne and nothynge worthe'. There were however a fair amount of livestock and arable land – 68 acres of standing corn, 97 acres of oats, 20 pigs, 5 cows, 125 sheep, 40 lambs, and 13 horses and mares 'for the plough'.

In March 1537, Francis Bedingfield obtained the lease of priory and lands; the site was granted to Sir William Fermer in 1546.

Hickling Priory

Hickling Priory (OS map reference TG 4182 2494) is the remains of a twelfth-century Augustinian priory. The ruins are on private land and are not open to the public.

The beginnings of the priory

The priory was founded in 1185 by Theobald, the son of Robert de Valoines. It was dedicated to the honour of St Mary, St Austin and All Saints.

Village sign at Hickling commemorating the priory.

When the building was completed, four canons from the Augustinian priory of St Osyth in Essex came to instruct the canons at Hickling in the rules of the order. The underlying principles of the Augustinians were that they had to live a common life, own no private property, and be concerned for the spiritual and material welfare of the people of the neighbourhood.

The terrible storm of December 1287

In 1287, there was a storm surge which caused major flooding in Hickling and the coast. The monastic chronicler John of Oxnead describes the flooding at Hickling and Horsey Gap as 'parts which no age in past times had recorded to have been covered by water'. The chroniclers Holinshed and Matthew of Westminster added that after heavy rain 'on the Feast of the Circumcision of our lord', the sea flowed over the land 'three or four leagues in breadth' from Yarmouth to the Humber and drowned cattle and knocked over buildings.

Over a hundred and eight people drowned in Hickling; in the priory, the water rose more than a foot above the high altar, and nearly all the canons fled for their lives. However, two of them remembered the rule of being concerned about material and spiritual welfare, and realised that the people left in the village would look to the priory for help when the waters receded. So they stayed behind; they managed to save the horses and other property by bringing them up into the dormitory over the vaulted undercroft.

Plague

In 1349, the prior, Richard de Hemsby, died of the plague. Just as the canons told the new successor, Simon Wodewale, that he'd been elected, Wodewale dropped dead from the plague. In the end, only two canons were left; and John, despite the fact that he was still only a novice, became the prior. In 1364, the pope allowed four of the canons to be ordained as priests, provided they'd reached the age of twenty-two, because the plague had meant that there were very few priests. Plague struck again in 1439, and three or four canons died.

Dilapidation, pirates and cudgels

The bell tower of the priory fell in 1400, and according to the Victorian scholar Henry Ellis (who edited the chronicle of John of Oxenedes), around the same time discipline in the priory started to become rather too relaxed. The monks apparently fought against some Flemish pirates who invaded and burned the village of Waxham in 1437; but when Bishop Goldwell did the visitation in 1492 and spoke to the prior, Thomas Gregg, and the eight canons, he was unhappy with what he found. The altars weren't covered properly and the vestments needed repair; not enough lamps were burning and there weren't enough fires in winter; the servants were badly paid; food and drink was scarce; and the priory didn't give enough treatments to the sick.

When Bishop Nix visited on 21 July 1514, the five canons said that all was well – though the prior admitted that he hadn't produced the accounts, Edward Norwich complained that the monks didn't attend daily services properly, and John Hickling complained that there was no schoolmaster. The bishop ordered that they had to have a grammar instructor by Christmas.

Bishop Nix visited again on 13 June 1532. John Hickling and Robert Aleyn said that the sick were being charged to attend the infirmary and Richard Norwich said that the steps to the hall were dangerously worn. The bishop ordered the priory to cover the costs of the sick attending the infirmary, and to and repair the steps. However, he also ordered something very unusual – he said that cudgels (*fustibus*) should be provided for the defence of the priory. The order is written in English as well as in Latin, so clearly it was thought to be very important.

It isn't clear who was thought to be attacking the priory – though the commissioners for the reformation attended very shortly. Thomas Legh and John Ap Rice wrote their usual scandalous report in 1536, claiming that Robert Walsham, Robert Allen, Robert Bastwick, John Michael and Matthew Wood were guilty of incontinency (in other words, they didn't keep their vow of celibacy), but the priory had been dissolved before the king's commissioners came to visit.

The end of the priory

The priory was dissolved in 1536, and the lands were given to William Rugge, the

Bishop of Norwich. The priory itself was granted to Sir William Wodehouse in 1542. A sarcophagus from the priory lies in Hickling church.

Sarcophagus from Hickling Priory, now in Hickling church.

Spooks: the tunnel and the balancing act

As usual, there is a tale of an underground passage attached to the priory. This particular tunnel is allegedly haunted by the ghost of a monk who walks the ruins and the marshes. He appears from the passage holding a parchment and quill, and apparently went mad while trying to balance the priory books.

The giant of Hickling

In 1826, some of the priory foundations were removed and the labourers found two stone coffins found; one was broken and the other was undisturbed. One of the labourers, expecting to find treasure, broke open the coffin and was shocked to find an entire skeleton inside – a skeleton which measured 6ft 4ins long, a good 9 inches taller than the average medieval man. The bones and coffin were apparently placed in Catfield church.

St Benet's Abbey, Horning

The remains of St Benet's Abbey are mainly the late fourteenth-century gatehouse with a windmill within its walls, plus fragments of the church, the fishponds and the crenellated walls. The gatehouse lies off St Benet's Road between Horning and Ludham – OS grid reference TG 381 159 – but it's easiest to reach it by boat.

The origins of the abbey

The abbey was originally founded on an island called Cowholm arund the year 800. According to the eighteenth-century historian Francis Blomefield (taking his information from Dugdale's *Monasticon Anglicanum*, which in turn takes its information from the chronicle of John of Brompton in the late fourteenth century), the original abbey was built by Suleman and was destroyed by the Danes in 870.

The current remains are part of the Benedictine foundation that was rebuilt by Wolfric and seven companions, who apparently lived there for sixty years until King Cnut found out they were there (allegedly through a vision), took them under his wing and endowed the monastery in 1020.

Remains of the gatehouse of St Benet's Abbey at Horning.

The abbey wasn't actually dissolved, making it the only abbey in England to escape the Dissolution. The Bishop of Norwich is therefore also the Abbot of St Benet's, and visits the abbey every August to hold an open-air service.

The estate is owned by Norfolk Archaeological Trust and is open to the public.

The moving church, 1160s

In the 1160s, Avelina de Ria moved the church of St Helen's – incredibly, one piece at a time, with the protection of armed guards – across the churchyard so that it was on her land and not the abbey's. Then she made people on the abbey lands pay tithes to the church (i.e. to her). William Turbe, the bishop of Norwich, ruled that she had to give the church back; she didn't, so the abbey complained to Henry II. Eventually, after a ruling from the king in their favour, the abbey installed their own priest in the church somewhere between 1164 and 1168. Avelina's reaction isn't recorded!

The runaway monk and the devil

According to Ernest Suffling, in his *History and Legends of the Broad District* (1891), a young monk ran away from the abbey and became profligate. The devil was about to carry him off when St Benet appeared, fought with devil and took the monk back to St Benet's. He gives an example of a twelfth-century woodcut illustrating the story with St Benet fighting the monk; the eighteenth-century historian Francis Blomefield says this is a seal from the monastery. In the illustration the devil has no horns, but it holds the monk in a huge beak, has a tail and hind legs like a lion's, and has truly fearsome claws and wings.

The floods of 1287

There was a major storm surge on 31 December 1287 (see Hickling Priory, page 59), and St Benet's was badly affected. The outbuildings were flooded to the point that they could only be reached by boat, and the horses were only saved by being brought into the nave of the church.

Clashes in Antingham, 1316

The abbot of St Benet's had major problems with one of the nearby lords of the manor in 1316. When the abbot sent Roger de Neatishead to Erpingham on priory business, Roger de Antyngham ambushed the monk at Southfield, dragged him through the fields, and rather horribly cut off the tail of his horse. De Antyngham's men also surrounded the abbot's manor at Antingham so the priory servants couldn't work or take food to the abbot at St Benet's.

When a groom rode the abbot's horse through the town, de Antyngham seized the horse with its saddle and starved it; he also took another of the abbot's horses on the road through North Walsham. Further, he took the abbot's plough-cattle at Antingham so the abbot's servants couldn't cultivate the land – and threatened the servants until they fled. However, things seemed to settle down again until the country rose in revolt in 1381 (see North Elmham Cathedral, page 91, for more details of the background to the rising).

The Rising of 1381

Apparently, the abbot of St Benet's was stricter than most in his insistence on feudal servie. On 20 June, a mob from Ludham and Potter Heigham, led by led by John-atte-Chaumbre, Adam Martyn and Henry Ryse, went to the abbey. Ryse had been one of the men who had killed Sir Robert Salle at Norwich, a few days before, so he had a very frightening reputation. The mob forced the abbot to surrender his court rolls – the records of fees and services owed to the abbey – which they then burned outside the abbey gate.

Three days later, there was a rumour that Henry Despenser, the 'fighting bishop' of Norwich, was on his way, so the rebels went back to St Benet's. According to some chroniclers, there was an all-night battle, but there is no evidence of arms or casualties on either side. Clearly it was frightening for the abbey; refugee monks from St Edmunds were staying there and had told the monks of St Benet's that John de Cambridge, the prior of the abbey at Bury St Edmunds, had been beheaded and his body lay in fields because nobody dared to retrieve it and bury it. Given these events and the recent deaths in Norwich, it's unsurprising that the monks feared for their lives. Apparently, they watched all night – but when the rebels discovered that the bishop wasn't there they left in peace.

The following September, there was a plot to take the abbey and use it as base for another revolt, but the authorities found out and beheaded the ringleaders on 20 October before anything happened.

After the rising had been suppressed, the abbot made copies of the court rolls. Although he didn't raise the rents, he insisted on a fine and an oath of allegiance from everyone who wanted their parcels of land back.

Gladman's Insurrection, 1443

The abbot of St Benet's ended up having a huge row with the citizens of Norwich when the new mills were built on the River Wensum. He claimed that they were damaging his mills – and the row ended up in a riot in Norwich known as Gladman's Insurrection. (See Norwich Cathedral on page 107 for the full story.)

Scandals...

The bishop's visitations – the inspection to check whether life in the religious institutions was proceeding as it should be – threw up some very interesting complaints, as well as a few scandals.

In July 1494 visitation, it was alleged that lay people entered the abbey and the monks' dormitory by day and night, silence wasn't observed properly in the choir, the younger monks were impudent and the servants were insolent. It was even claimed that the abbey jewels had been pawned by Robert Wynbarrow, who refused to get them back. Plus the previous abbot had given the vicarage of St Peter's in Hoveton to one of his own relative; the current abbot, Robert Cubitt, had too many servants; and the monks' tasks were so burdensome and rigorous that they had no time for study.

In 1514, almost half of the monks said *'omnia bene'* (i.e. all was well) – but then the monk John Rising admitted there was a conspiracy among the monks to say nothing. Robert Cowper, the subprior, said he'd lost two pieces of silver plate and two masers (large cups). The monks accused John Redyng, the prior, of not getting up in time for matins (early morning services), and said that he allowed women into his official chambers and he was suspected of being unchaste. He also retained a few offices such as cellarer, sacrist, and almoner for himself, and didn't present any accounts. The bishop ordered him to present his accounts on St Clement's Day (23 November) and three monks should be elected to help him prepare the accounts; an inventory of the goods had to be made; and Robert Cowper had to pay £4, at the rate of 20 shillings a year (the equivalent of almost £1,800 or £445 a year in modern terms), to make good any losses.

John Salcot took over as abbot in 1517 after Redyng's death; he revived discipline, took the finances in hand and started to reduce the monastery's debt. The 1520 visitation went reasonably well – but things had slipped again by 1526. The complaints included that there were too many dogs in the monastery precinct (owned by Thomas Stonham, who loved hunting), the altar cloths were grubby, and not enough was done for the sick. One monk was singled out for attention: William Bynham always claimed he was sick so he couldn't get up for matins, but everyone knew he was perfectly well and he ate and drank as much as everyone else. The bishop ruled that the dogs shouldn't have scraps from the table, which should be given to the poor, better attention should be paid to the sick, and the altar cloths should be kept clean. As for Bynham: the bishop intended to put him in prison at Norwich, but the abbot stepped in and asked him not to. The bishop agreed, but warned that if Bynham was disobedient in future he would be sent to Norwich and put in prison.

In 1532, discipline was even worse. William Repps (aka William Rugge) was the prior, and he told the bishop, '*Omnia bene,*' – but the monks told the bishop the truth. Some of the monks used boots instead of sandals (though the abbot was let off this offence because he claimed to have a disease of the shins). The prior didn't get up for matins and neglected his offices, and the third prior went hunting straight after matins; the church vestments and ornaments were in poor condition; and the monks didn't get their pittances (pocket money) regularly. In addition, the abbey was in debt to the tune of £600 12s 5¾d (the equivalent to almost a quarter of a million pounds in terms of today's money). The bishop kept the visitation open for six months to give the abbey a chance to improve, but his injunctions aren't recorded.

… and spooks

There are two ghost stories involving the priory.

The first ghost is allegedly seen every 25 May, on the anniversary of a dark deed. The folklorist Enid Porter says that Ethelwold was a monk who'd been sent on an errand and had been captured by the Normans. The Normans promised to make him abbot if he opened the gate; he did so, and most of the monks were slain. When Ethelwold asked for his reward, they dressed him as an abbot – then hanged him from the beam above the abbey gateway.

However, there isn't any evidence for the story. The second abbot of St Benet's, Thurtan de Ludham, was responsible for much of the stone building and died in

1064; his successor, Ethelwold, is described by John de Oxenedes as prudent and honourable – hardly the sort who would betray his fellow monks. Also, Ethelwold was alive well after 1066; despite arguments with William the Conqueror, he remained abbot of St Benet's until his death in 1089.

The second tale is much sadder – that of Brother Pacificus. The story goes that he was an incredibly skilled artist who'd spent weeks repairing the rood screen at Ranworth. Every morning at dawn he'd row the two miles to Ranworth, and every evening when the sun began to set he'd row back to the Abbey. But one evening when he returned to the Abbey, he found it empty and silent: he discovered that it had been sacked by Henry VIII's soldiers and all the other monks had been killed. Broken-hearted, Pacificus then became a hermit in the ruins, and he still rows a boat along that stretch of the Broads with his dog sitting in it.

Again, the evidence for this is scant: the Abbey wasn't dissolved and none of the monks were killed. However, people have seen a mysterious figure sailing silently with his dog…

The saints of St Benet's

According to Claude Messent, two saints were buried at St Benet's. The first is St Wolfey (or Wolfeius), who was the first hermit of St Benet's and was buried there. The second is St Margaret the Martyr; very little is known of her, other than that she was killed in Little Wood in Hoveton on 22 May 1170, and was buried under the high altar of the abbey church – who killed her and why is unknown.

The Ludham dragon

There is a legend in Ludham that a monster, much like a dragon, made its burrow in a street by the church. The villagers waited for it to come out, one day, and then blocked the entrance with stones so the dragon couldn't get back in. It duly stomped over to the Abbey, where it entered the vaults and stayed there.

Detail of rood screen from St Helen's church, Ranworth – St George conquering the dragon.

Interestingly, there is an article in the *Norfolk Chronicle* from 28 September 1782, which says that Jasper Andrews killed an enormous snake at Ludham on Monday 16 September. The snake was apparently 5 feet 8 inches long, almost 3 feet in circumference, and had a 'very long snout'. It also had two 'execrescences' (bumps) on its head which were like horns (making the snake very dragon-like in appearance). It only came out at night and had several burrows, including one near the bake-office, one at the rectory, and one at Ludham Hall. The newspaper added that the skin was in the possession of Mr J. Garrett, a wealthy farmer in the neighbourhood.

Tunnels

Allegedly there is an underground tunnel running between the abbey and the church of St Helen's at Ranworth. It's said that lots of treasure is buried in the tunnel, guarded by the ghost of a huge dog. And someone digging in a neighbouring garden found a culvert – although it was merely a drainage system, the find added to the rumours!

Dissolution... or not

Ap Rice and Legh visited St Benet's in 1535 and claimed that four of the monks admitted to being unchaste. They also said that the monks had a conspiracy of silence.

However, a couple of months later, Henry VIII chose the abbot (William Rugge) to be the bishop of Norwich. Under an Act of Parliament, the bishop of Norwich's

St Helen's church, Ranworth.

possessions were given to the king in exchange for the abbey of St Benet... and the abbey was never actually dissolved. William Rugge remained the Abbot of St Benet's as well as being the Bishop of Norwich – and continued to live an extravagant lifestyle. In 1550, he had to resign as bishop in exchange for his debts being written off.

Although the Act of Parliament said that at least twelve monks and a prior should stay at St Benet's to keep divine service, the last monks had left by 1545 and the building fell into decay. Some of the stone was used to build the Duke of Norfolk's palace in Norwich (itself pulled down in the early 1700s).

By 1585 the abbey was in ruins. Edmund Dye (or Dey), a fisherman, had a lodge in the grounds; the house became the Chequers pub and then a private house, but burned down in 1891.

The brick mill was built in the gatehouse somewhere between 1728 and 1735, and is the earliest brick mill in Norfolk. It was originally used to crush colza seeds (i.e. oilseed rape) for oil lamps, and was converted to a drainage mill in the 1800s. It stopped being used 1863 when its cap blew off in a gale.

The ruins themselves were partly removed in 1840; stained glass, a stone coffin and a skull in a vessel were found.

St Faith's Priory, Horsham

The priory of St Faith's in Horsham was founded in 1105 by Robert Fitzwalter, Lord of Horsford and Horsham, and his wife Sibyl, daughter and heiress of Ralph de Cheney. It was a Benedictine priory dedicated to St Faith, and was known as an alien priory as it was a cell of the abbey at Conques. The only remains are the monastery refectory, which is part of the house built behind the church in Horsham St Faiths (OS map reference TG 2166 1517).

However, the remains are absolutely stunning, because there is a series of incredible wall paintings which show the whole story behind the building of the monastery.

Captured by brigands

Robert and Sibyl Fitzwalter were very devout, and had been on a pilgrimage to Rome. On their way back, they were travelling

Wall painting of St Faith in the priory remains at Horsham St Faith's.

through France when they were captured by brigands – clearly on the lookout for wealthy pilgrims – and taken to the pirates' stronghold, where they were chained in prison.

As all devout pilgrims would, Robert and Sibyl prayed: firstly to God, and then to St Faith. (St Faith was a virgin martyr – horribly, she was roasted to death on a bed and then beheaded. Soldiers, prisoners and pilgrims prayed to her.) St Faith appeared to them in a vision, loosened their chains, and brought them out of the prison – though she left their fetters in place. Robert and Sibyl made their way to the shrine of St Faith in Conques and offered up their fetters, along with their tale.

While they rested and recovered at the abbey, Robert and Sibyl read about the life of St Faith, and vowed that when they returned to their manor at Horsford they would build a monastery, a cell to the abbey of Conques, and it would be dedicated to St Faith. Two of the monks from Conques, Barnard and Girard, returned to England with them to help them set up the monastery.

Spooks: building work stopped by devils

Building work began at 'Kirkescroft' in Horsford (clearly, from the name, this was an open space near to the church – and also near to the castle at Horsford, which belonged to the de Cheyney family). But, according to the version told in Dugdale's *Monasticon*, every morning when they went to continue the work, all the building that had been done the previous day had fallen down in the night. Robert and Sibyl believed that devils had taken down the building work, so instead they decided to build the monastery about a mile away at Horsham. To their relief, there were no problems with the building work and the priory was set up.

The story of the priory

The story of the founding was painted onto the walls of the refectory during the thirteenth century, but remained hidden behind Tudor panelling until the house

Wall painting in the priory remains at Horsham St Faith's, showing the monastery's founders being captured by pirates.

Wall painting in the priory remains at Horsham St Faith's, showing the monastery's founders being let of their prison by St Faith.

Wall painting in the priory remains at Horsham St Faith's, showing the monastery's founders returning by sea.

Wall painting in the priory remains at Horsham St Faith's, showing the monastery's founders building the priory as thanks to St Faith.

was renovated in 1968 and the paintings were rediscovered. The first two scenes are hidden by the north wall but show the sea voyage to the south of France. The third scene shows them on horseback, being captured by the pirates.

The fourth scene shows them in prison, the fifth scene shows them praying to St Faith, and the sixth scene shows St Faith opening the door of the prison.

Scene seven shows Robert and Sibyl kneeling before the abbot of Conques, and the eighth scene shows them sailing back to England with the two monks.

The final scene shows the priory being built – and it's so detailed that you can even see a man with a wheelbarrow.

Hospital and the Knights Templar

In the mid-twelfth century, Ralph de Granville built a hospital nearby for the Knights Templar. The pope gave the hospital to the priory in 1163.

The siege of 1307

Life wasn't particularly peaceful for the priory. On 1 December 1307, a commission was appointed to look into a complaint by the prior – that towards the end of the reign of the late king (i.e. Edward I, who died in July 1307) Robert de Barwe, Hubert le Warner and 25 others broke into the priory, ate all the food and used all the goods, then guarded the priory gates for four months. The prior couldn't get in – and the monks trapped inside couldn't get out.

Meanwhile de Barwe and his men carried off the prior's palfrey, worth 10 marks (£12 16s, or the equivalent of just over £5,000 in terms of today's money), killed seven pigs in the woods, worth 40 shillings (nearly £800 in terms of today's money), and threw a monk from his horse on the main road before carrying him off to Horsford, ruining his habit and shoes, and throwing him into prison. They also went into the prior's market in Horsham and collected the tolls as well as taking all the goods from the prior's servants.

They seized twelve carthorses and impounded them for a month; the horses would normally have been used to carry grain, but because the monks couldn't transport the grain they weren't able to harvest it, and the grain was trampled in the fields by cattle. The monks tried to carry some of the grain on their backs, but de Barwe's men waylaid a servant who was meant to gather the corn and threw him off his horse before taking the horse away. Furthermore, de Barwe felled the trees, smashed up the fences and closes, drove off the cattle, and hunted all the hares out of the prior's warren.

It's not immediately clear why the priory fell foul of de Barwe. However, given that England was at war with France and in 1307 the Cluniac priories had been ordered to stop sending money to Cluny, it could be that the monks at Horsham, being a cell of a French abbey, were seen as a legitimate target for patriotic men who didn't want money being sent to France and decided that thuggery was the required behaviour.

War

The priory continued, but it was struggling. They were classed as aliens (as they were a cell of a French abbey) during the Hundred Years' War, and had to pay £50 a year to the king (the equivalent of almost £22,000 in terms of today's money) as long as the war went on. By 1390, the monks were desperate, and begged to be naturalised because they simply couldn't afford to pay. They pleaded that they used to have a prior and twelve monks celebrating three masses daily, and gave every poor beggar a loaf and two herrings as well as other charitable duties; but in 1390 the monastery was almost in ruins, divine service had been abandoned, and they were reduced to a prior and eight monks. They could barely afford to feed themselves, let alone do the charitable duties they had pledged to do.

In the end, the king agreed to them paying a fine to become denizen (i.e. English). The priory in turn agreed that they would pay him the two marks a year they had previously paid to the abbey of Conques (£1, 12s and 8d or the equivalent of just over £700 in terms of today's money – a considerably lower sum than they had been paying), would pray every day for the king and queen, and their prior would be an Englishman rather than someone from Conques.

The end of the priory

Thomas Legh and John Ap Rice reported in 1535 that the house was large and two of the priors were keen to be dismissed. The prior, John Salisbury, wrote to the prior two days after their visit, complaining that they'd taken the movable goods without any just cause. The priory was dissolved in late 1536 and was sold to Sir Richard Southwell, one of the king's commissioners. Southwell demolished most of the priory and converted the refectory wing (the north range) into a private home for his mistress and their three children.

Tunnels

As with many religious houses, there's a story of an underground tunnel. The one at Horsham allegedly ran to the motte and bailey castle at Horsford – unsurprisingly, because the castle belonged to the de Cheyney family, Sibyl's family.

Robert Southwell, the Jesuit martyr

Although there are no ghost stories associated with the priory at Horsham, the place is linked to the story of a martyr. Sir Richard Southwell's grandson Robert, born at Horsham in 1561, was apparently so beautiful as a baby that the gipsies in the nearby woods couldn't resist stealing him. However, his nurse managed to recover the boy; he grew up to be a noted religious poet and martyr.

He was raised as a Catholic, even though his father was a protestant, and studied at Douai. He begged the Jesuit order to let him become a priest, but they refused because he was too young. Eventually, at the age of 17, he became a novice; two years later, in 1580, he studied at the Jesuit college in Rome. He was ordained in 1584 and returned to England with Henry Garnet in May 1586 to minister to Catholics, even though he knew that if he was caught he would be executed for treason. He called himself Mr Cotton and travelled widely in the south of England, celebrating mass and hiding at times for hours behind panelling. He settled in London and was chaplain to Anne, Countess of Arundel. He wrote many poems and tracts, and years later Ben Jonson said that he would have been happy to burn many of his own poems if he could have written Southwell's poem 'The Burning Babe'.

However, then William Cecil, the queen's chief adviser, issued 'A declaration of great troubles pretended against the realme by a number of seminarie priests and Jesuits'. Southwell wrote a response, *An Humble Supplication to Her Majestie*. It addresses each point in Cecil's tract and makes the point that the Jesuits' only concern was 'to labour for the salvation of soules, and in peaceable and quiet sort to confirme them in the auntient Catholique Faith'. It was circulated only in manuscript form as it was much too dangerous to publish – but Cecil undoubtedly knew of it and wanted Southwell stopped.

On 25 June 1592, Southwell was travelling to Warwickshire with his friend Thomas Bellamy, but stopped to say mass at the Bellamys' house at Uxenden, near Harrow. Thomas's sister Anne betrayed Southwell to the priest-hunter Richard Topcliffe, and Southwell was caught. Although he called himself 'Mr Cotton', his red hair was distinctive and Topcliffe knew exactly who he'd caught.

Southwell was tortured before being thrown into a prison cell in the gatehouse of the Tower of London for a month. His father visited and was shocked to see the state of his son, filthy and covered in lice; he appealed to Elizabeth I (Robert's mother had been Elizabeth's governess), and the queen had Southwell moved to a clean cell at the end of July. His family were allowed to visit and give him clean clothes, a Bible and books; he was also allowed to write poetry. He was held in tower for three years and refused to betray his fellow Catholics, despite being tortured 13 times.

He was put in the underground cell (known as Limbo) in Newgate Gaol, awaiting trial, in February 1595. He still refused to betray his fellow Catholics, and was sentenced to be hanged, drawn and quartered as a traitor. He was sent to Tyburn on 21 February 1595 (though mercifully was dead before the second part of his sentence was carried out) and was canonised as a martyr in 1970.

The Trinitarian Priory of Ingham

Ingham Priory is the remains of a fourteenth-century Trinitarian priory, interlocked with the north side of Holy Trinity church in Ingham (OS map reference TG 3910 2604). There are also traces of the cloister archways inside the church to the north of the nave. Like the church, it is open to the public.

Remains of Ingham Priory.

The beginnings of the priory

The priory was founded in 1360 by Sir Miles Stapleton of Bedale, Yorkshire. Because he married Joan, the younger daughter and only surviving child of Oliver de Ingham, Miles decided to build the priory in her family's village rather than in Yorkshire. Sir Oliver had rebuilt the church just after the Black Death, so Miles built a monument to Sir Oliver de Ingham and his wife Elizabeth in the church. Originally, the monument was richly coloured, and two angels held Sir Oliver's helmet, although the angels were damaged presumably during the Reformation. Writing at the end of the nineteenth century, Ernest Suffling said that Oliver's helmet was showing 'alarming signs of decay' and suggested that a coat of Vaseline was needed. In 1613, the helmet was recorded as having the crest of an owl and a thorn bush.

This also a space on the floor next to the monument that originally housed brasses to Sir Miles and Joan; on the wall, there is a copy based on a rubbing taken several centuries ago, and it's recorded that the figures were 68½ inches long.

The priory is unusual because it was part of the Order of the Holy Trinity and St Victor for the Redemption of Captives, which was founded in 1198. Only 12 houses of this order were found in England, and Ingham was the last of them to be founded. It was however briefly the head of the order in England, and it's the only Trinitarian house in

Sir Oliver de Ingham lying on a bed of pebbles in the nave of Ingham church.

England with any surviving buildings, as well as being the only Trinitarian priory in East Anglia (the next nearest one is in Hertfordshire). The Swan Inn, next to the church, was part of the priory before the dissolution of the monasteries.

The name 'Trinitarian' came about because the followers of the order divided their possessions into three. One part was to be used for the redemption of captives (Christians who had fallen into the hands of infidels, i.e. Saracens, during the Crusades), one part for the poor, and one part for themselves.

The original priory had merely one prior and two canons, but eventually four other canons joined them, along with a sacrist. The sacrist lived in two rooms above the church porch and also officiated for the parishioners, who shared the church with the order.

Scandals and dissolution

The visitations gave fairly good reports of the priory; in 1520 the prior, Thomas Catfield, admitted to failing to do the accounts, and was told to give a set of accounts by Michaelmas. In 1526 the report was *'omnia bene'*.

According to Ernest Suffling, the priory was suppressed mainly because of 'the amours of the prior, John Say, with the village lasses'. However, there's no record of this in the records of the bishop's visitation of 1532. Although Thomas Legh and John Ap Rice alleged that the prior and one of the monks were guilty of incontinence (in other words, they didn't keep their vow of celibacy), they said exactly the same about other monks and nuns who were perfectly blameless, so their accounts can be taken with a pinch of salt.

The priory was due to be dissolved in 1536 – and there was a huge row in 1535 because the prior sold the house and lands to William Woodhouse at the end of the previous without knowledge or consent of the priory's patron, Sir Francis

Calthrope. Meanwhile, the king's commissioners had promised to offer the priory to Sir Francis's heir, Edward Calthrope. Woodhouse was summoned in front of the commissioners and argued that it was a house of Crossed Friars and not of monks or canons, so the prior was at liberty to sell to him. Somehow the argument worked, because Woodhouse kept the property and exchanged it for Hickling Priory in 1544.

Gravel quarrying destroyed much of the priory site.

Spooks: the dancing monks, the tunnel, and the fighting knights

Ghosts of dancing monks have been seen at the priory, apparently after bones were disturbed during the Dissolution.

Ernest Suffling, in his *History and Legends of the Broads District* (1891), says that the church altar was taken down for repairs in the 1860s and nineteen skeletons were found beneath it, along with a tunnel linking the priory with the manor house. However, the tunnel was never explored and was sealed up again.

Charles Sampson, in his *Ghosts of the Broads* (1931), claims that there are other ghosts associated with the church. And the story's very reminiscent of Edith Nesbit's wonderful ghost story *Man-Size in Marble*. According to Sampson, every 3 June (though other sources name the date as 2 August), Sir Oliver de Ingham's and Sir Roger de Bois's stone images on their tombs become flesh and walk together down to Stalham Broad before doing battle with a Middle Eastern figure. When they have slain their enemy, they walk back to the church, lie down on their tombs again, and stay there… until the next anniversary.

Rather gruesomely, Sir Roger de Bois doesn't have a pillow on which to rest his head, unlike his wife Margaret; instead, he uses the decapitated head of a former enemy!

Close up of Sir Roger de Bois resting his head on his 'pillow' of a decapitated head in Ingham church.

Greyfriars Tower, King's Lynn

Greyfriar's Tower off St James' Street in King's Lynn (OS map reference TF 6202 1976) is a lantern tower which is the remains of a thirteenth-century friary. It's said to be the best surviving example of a Mendicant tower with a passageway in the country.

The beginnings of the friary

The friary was founded in 1264 by Thomas Feltham in Fuller's Lane for a group for Franciscan friars. It was enlarged in 1364 – the tower dates from then – and was suppressed in October 1538. The site was sold to John Eyre, one of the king's commissioners; he also bought the lands of the other friaries in Lynn.

The tower remained because it was used as a seamark by traders and sailors navigating The Wash. It was known as the 'leaning tower of Lynn' – however, the degree of lean is much less than that at Pisa, being 1 degree rather than 5.5 degrees.

The gardens around it were laid out in 1911 to mark the coronation of George V. It was a finalist in the first series of the BBC2 television series *Restoration*, and the restoration was finished in October 2006.

The plague

A chronicle of the Grey Friars at Lynn exists from the fourteenth century, and it actually talks about the beginning of the Black Death in England:

> In this year, 1348, in Melcombe in the county of Dorset, a little before the feast of St John the Baptist, two ships, one of them from Bristol, came alongside. One of the sailors had brought from them from Gascony the seeds of the terrible pestilence, and through him the men of that town of Melcombe were the first in England to be infected.

Tunnels and spooks

As is often the case with religious establishments, there's a legend of a mysterious tunnel leading from the priory. Actually, Greyfriars Priory allegedly has two tunnels. One leads to the Red Mount Chapel; and one leads to the White Hart pub in St James' Street, which is supposedly haunted by a monk. Tantalisingly, there are no details of when the monk appears or what he does.

More prosaically, any tunnel is likely to have been a water conduit; in 1314 the house was granted a licence to retain a mill called 'Buckenwell' in North Runcton

Greyfriars Tower, King's Lynn, plate from Thomas Kitson
Cromwell's Excursions Through Norfolk, *volume 2, 1819.*

(the friars had bought it from Thomas Bardolf without permission from the king)
and to 'lead the water from the well by an underground conduit to their house in
Lynn'.

Langley Abbey

Remains of Langley Abbey, plate from Thomas Kitson Cromwell's
Excursions Through Norfolk, *1819 .*

L angley Abbey is the remains of a twelfth-century Premonstratensian abbey (OS map reference TG 3624 0291). The remains are used as farm buildings and the abbey is not open to the public. Pevsner notes that in the surviving buildings there is a lavatorium, with a boss showing an eagle clasping a bird.

The beginnings of the abbey

The abbey was founded in 1195 by Sir Robert FitzRoger Helke, Lord of Horsford (was sheriff of Norfolk and Suffolk in 1192) and was dedicated to the honour of the Blessed Virgin. It was set up for an abbot and 15 canons, chosen from the priory of Alnwick.

The Premonstratensians were also known as White Canons (as they wore a white habit) and were sometimes called Norbertines, because they were founded by St Norbert of Xanten at Prémontré in France. They followed the Augustine rule but observed a slightly stricter lifestyle.

The abbot was granted a licence to crenellate in 1346 but, as the patent rolls say it was for a new belfry only, it's clear that the abbey wasn't being altered to be a defensive building.

Tax collecting

The abbot of Langley was the collector for the crusade tenth for the diocese of Norwich. He duly paid £200 to the king's clerk and got a receipt on 10 February 1304.

In 1305, he sent around £200, and in 1306 he sent £229, 11 shillings and 6 pence. However, the abbot and his clerk, Thomas de Jernemuta, had been taken to court at Westminster, because various clerics claimed that they'd paid the tax but the abbot had listed them as being in arrears. The king appointed Walter de Norwich to examine the accounts and certify to the auditors.

Scandals and 'evil living'

The bishop's visitation of 1478 found that discipline was poor as the abbot was very old and ill. One monk, Thomas Russell, was accused of 'evil living'; he was sentenced to bread and water for 40 days and then banished for three years to another house. Two other monks went out of the abbey without leave from the abbot, and were also sentenced to penance of bread and water for 40 days. Interestingly, the bishop gave an injunction that no doors were ever to be fastened to stop the superior entering, and he also banned any recreation outside the abbey precincts.

At his next visit, in 1482, the monks were still behaving scandalously; this time, the bishop added that the inns outside the abbey were out of bounds, which clearly tells us what the monks were doing in their free time! In addition, nobody was to leave the precincts unless they were performing a divine service in church. The abbot, John Myntyng, was accused of incontinence (i.e. lack of chastity) and waste, and his powers were temporarily transferred to two canons under the Abbot of Wendling.

Things had improved by the bishop's next visit, in 1486, and the abbey's debt had halved – but there were clearly still some problems as the bishop banned hunting or fishing by night, and made a point of mentioning that anyone who left the monastery without leave would be excommunicated.

However, the real scandal was in 1491, when Canon Thomas Ludham had cut off a man's right hand in a fight. (The reason for the argument isn't clear.) He was sentenced to 40 days' penance (bread and water, as usual), and then to be exiled to Sulham where he would be in perpetual imprisonment.

However, although there are records of Thomas being at Sulham in 1494, in 1497 he's listed as the subprior at Langley, so clearly he was forgiven (though it's also notable that the bishop stayed for three days – much longer than usual, and probably as part of a punishment for the lax behaviour of the monks).

William Curlew was elected bishop in 1500 but was forced to resign two years later for 'delinquencies' – and he was summoned to the provincial chapter at Nottingham in 1503 to answer questions about the state of his soul, threatened with excommunication if he didn't turn up.

Dissolution

Langley Abbey was dissolved in 1536, and the revenues were granted to John Berney.

The Ranworth Antiphoner

The monks produced a 285-page antiphoner book on sheepskin, with the psalms and responses for each of the seven services held every day of year. (The name comes from the fact that the priest and the congregation speak alternately or 'antiphonally'.) The canons from Langley were the vicars of Ranworth, and used the service book at St Helen's church in Ranworth. It was bequeathed to Ranworth in 1478 by John Cobbe; however, in 1549, because it was in Latin and the Prayer Book of 1549 said that services had to be in English, it wasn't allowed to be used. It disappeared for 300 years, when it was found in a private collection. When it finally came on the market, the bookseller sold it to Ranworth church for the amount he'd paid for it – £575. The money was raised by subscription (the equivalent of over £40,000, in today's money) and the Antiphoner returned to Ranworth in 1912.

Detail of antiphoher at St Helen's church, Ranworth.

Ghosts and tunnels

There was a cross at Langley which marked the boundaries of the parishes of Langley, Chedgrave, Thurton and Carleton St. Peter. According to W. A. Dutt in *The Norfolk Broads* (1905, 2nd edition), there was a legend that the cross had a curse on it; if it was moved, then Langley Hall would burn down. In 1801, the cross was moved by Lady Beauchamp – and the turret of the hall did indeed catch fire (although it was quickly extinguished).

Abbey Farm burned down in 1801 (and the cross was moved into the park afterwards by Sir Thomas Beauchamp Proctor – rather more prosaically than the legend!). Apparently, workers among the ruins found a tunnel which was bigger than a sewer but nobody would dare go down it. Another legend says that the tunnel leads to a chapel underneath Ranworth Broad, and you can hear ghosts of monks chanting beneath it on quiet nights.

St Edmund's Chapel, Lyng

St Edmund's Chapel, Lyng lies in a field just off Easthaugh Road in Lyng (OS map reference TG 0781 1732), and the masonry and arch are the only remains of the Benedictine Nunnery. The date of the nunnery's foundation is unknown, but it was dissolved in 1176 when it moved to Thetford (see page 132).

The mysterious silver chalice and the drowned bells

According to folklorist Enid Porter, there was once a drainage channel from the River Wensum which ran under St Edmund's chapel. Two watermen fished a silver chalice out of the river, and an argument started about who should keep it. One of the watermen swore at the other – and the chalice immediately jumped into the air, fell back into the water and was never seen again.

Remains of St Edmund's Chapel, Lyng.

Another legend focuses on the bells of the nunnery. The tradition goes that when the nunnery closed, the bells were thrown into the river – and the bells could still be heard ringing, on some nights.

Spooks and headless horsemen

Opposite the field containing the nunnery ruins is a footpath which goes from Easthaugh Road to Collen's Green, known as the King's Grove. It's rumoured to be the site of a battle between St Edmund and the Danes, and nearby fields actually had the names 'Upper Prisoners' Close' and 'Lower Prisoners' Close'. Edmund's forces were defeated and driven back to Castle Acre, and the ghosts of the dead soldiers allegedly still haunt the grove. Other sources say that headless horses can be seen there, too – and children were allegedly let out from school twenty minutes early in the winter in the mid-nineteenth century so they didn't have to pass the area in the dark. When the road on Hoggsbeck Hill was excavated, skeletons were unearthed; it's not clear whether they were indeed the bones of ancient warriors or whether they were from the graveyard of the former nunnery, but again the children were let out early from school so they didn't have to pass the site in the dark.

The Great Stone of Lyng

Halfway up the King's Grove is the Great Stone of Lyng, a toad-shaped boulder. Many stories are told about it – no birds sing near it; treasure is buried beneath it; and, on certain (unspecified) nights, the stone bleeds if pricked with a pin, because of the blood it absorbed from Edmund's soldiers. (Another legend claims that the blood comes from sacrificial victims of the druids.)

So tradition goes, one landowner allegedly wanted the boulder as decoration for his park – though it's just as likely that he wanted the legendary treasure beneath it. So he harnessed between eight and a dozen horses, thinking that they'd be able to shift the stone. The stone moved very slightly, then sank even deeper, and the landowner had to give up.

The stone is actually an 'erratic', i.e. a boulder deposited by glaciers in the Ice Age. In ancient times, these boulders used to be moved to mark meeting places or boundaries, and the stories told about such stones usually include buried treasure, or the fact that the stone grows or moves.

The Great Stone of Lyng. Chloë, aged 7, was 1m 40cm tall at the time of the photograph, taken by author.

When we visited it, the stone seemed particularly toadlike as it was covered in moss; the 'eyes' and the 'mouth' are easily traceable. Although we heard the birds singing (disproving that particular myth), the walk up King's Grove was quite eerie – particularly when a deer bounded across our path not more than ten metres in front of us…

Marham Abbey

Remains of the abbey at Marham.

Marham Abbey is the remains of a thirteenth-century Cistercian nunnery (OS map reference TF 706 098). There are some remains of buildings and a large fishpond in the grounds of Abbey House on Shouldham Road (which is not open to the public), but the buried footings of the site can be seen in the field opposite the church.

The beginnings of the abbey

The abbey was founded by Isabel, the widow of Hugh d'Albini, earl of Arundel, and had between 10 and 15 nuns. In January 1249 it was dedicated to the honour of the Blessed Virgin, St Barbara, and St Edmund by Richard, the bishop of Chichester. In 1252 it was formally incorporated into the Cistercian abbey at Waverley.

A fight with the king

In 1252, a row blew up between Isabel and Henry III, when the king took custody of a deceased tenant's estate. The estate included a quarter of a knight's fee, the wardship of which belonged to Isobel. Isobel asked the king to give it back – and he refused. According to the monastic chronicler Matthew Paris (who was clearly close to Isobel because he translated some of his own work for her into Anglo-Norman verse, as well as arranging the loan of other books), Isabel took the king to court and denounced him to his face for being untrustworthy, saying that the rules in the Magna Carta would be very easily broken. Paris even gives her a dramatic speech: 'Where are the liberties of England, so often recorded, so often granted, and so often ransomed?'

Although Paris then says that Isabel left the court without her part of the wardship, records show that a year later the king did indeed return the wardship – and he also let Isobel off having the pay the fine of 35 marks (£21, 12s and 8d, or the equivalent of nearly £7,000 in terms of today's money) that she'd had to pay in order to appeal her case.

Isabel died in November 1282 and was buried at Marham.

Poverty

Despite Isabel's generosity, the abbey was seen as so poor that in 1291 it was exempt from paying tithes. Interestingly, the prioress had the right to keep gallows.

Scandal and dissolution

Thomas Legh and John Ap Rice, in their 'scandalous comperta', had plenty to say about the nuns of Marham in 1536. Usually, their views can be taken with a pinch of salt – but in the case of Marham they really did have a point when they said that the abbess, Barbara Mason, and four of her nuns had confessed to grave incontinency (in other words, they hadn't kept their vow of celibacy). The county commissioners, who were much more sober, visited Marham in the same year and stated that there were:

> Religious persons of slaunderous Reporte whereof iij of them doue require ther Dispensacions, and the residue wyll contynue in Religione.

The commissioners also mentioned that the house was in a poor state. The house was dissolved in 1536, the goods were sold in 1537, and a lease of the site was granted to Thomas Bukworth, serjeant-at-arms. In 1546 the site of the abbey was granted to Sir Nicholas Hare of London.

Ghosts

Marham doesn't have a tunnel legend – instead, their ghost involves a bricked-up nun, Sister Barbara. It's not clear if she's meant to be identified as Barbara, the last abbess of Marham – and I should add here that nuns were never bricked up behind walls at Marham, so part of the story is definitely untrue. But the rest of

Village sign at Marham commemorating the abbey and Sister Barbara (top right).

the story's quite a good one...

Sister Barbara made huge amounts of money for the abbey because she was so good to travellers, nursing them back to health. The monks of Pentney weren't happy that she was making so much money, and they were also suspicious about the number of travellers who were injured – so they spied on her. And their discovery was shocking: Sister Barbara paid ruffians to stop rich merchants on Vinegar Hill (on the main road from King's Lynn to Swaffham) and knock them out. The ruffians then gave the riches to Barbara (after taking their cut, of course), and she sallied forth to tend to poor injured traveller and nurse him back to health at the abbey. In gratitude for her help (and having no idea that she was the cause behind his injuries), the traveller would give gifts to the monastery.

The monks at Pentney were known for their charity and good works (see page 116); once their story became public knowledge, Sister Barbara was swiftly brought to justice. She was bricked up behind a wall in the nunnery and left to starve to death. Now her ghost allegedly walks the path up to Vinegar Hill on bright nights in November.

One place she definitely walks is on the village signpost (top right, above):

New Buckenham Castle

Remains of Buckenham Castle.

New Buckenham castle is actually just inside the parish boundary of Old Buckenham, on Castle Road (OS map reference TM 08454 90399). The key to the castle is available at the garage on Castle Road during opening hours.

The castle before the castle...

The story of New Buckenham castle actually starts in Old Buckenham. There was originally a wooden castle there, just off Abbey Road, which belonged to Ralph Guader in the time of Edward the Confessor. However, after Ralph's rebellion (see Norwich Castle, page 98), William the Conqueror divided Ralph's lands among his tenants in chief and gave Old Buckenham castle to William d'Albini, a Norman baron who was also the king's butler.

William was succeeded by his son, also named William, who decided to build himself a new castle two miles away to the south-west after his marriage to Adelize (or Adelais), the dowager queen of Henry I, in 1138. So he obtained a licence to build a new castle in 1140, started building New Buckenham Castle in around 1145, and gave the site of Old Buckenham Castle to the Augustinian canons in 1146.

His grant expressly said that he was giving the monks the site of the castle, which was to be destroyed, and eighty acres of land: *'cum sede castelli lxxx acras et castellum diruendum'*. The castle was destroyed, and a priory was built on the west

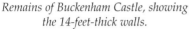

Remains of Buckenham Castle, showing the 14-feet-thick walls.

Buckenham Castle, plate from Thomas Kitson Cromwell's Excursions Through Norfolk, *vol II, 1819.*

side of the castle, dedicated to the honour of God, St Mary, St James, and All Saints.

There are very few remains of Old Buckenham castle or the priory – a few lumps of flint and rubble, and a wet ditch belonging to the original earth ringwork fortress. Henry Harrod, writing in 1857, said that the old castle was built on a Roman camp, the banks of the castle enclosed the priory garden, and the only trace left of the destroyed castle was a portion of a stone sewer into the ditch on the north side.

Old Buckenham Priory – scandals

The story of the priory is fairly quiet, although there were some scandals uncovered during the Episcopal visitations. In 1492, the canons complained that Jon Bukenham, the prior, didn't keep accounts and didn't take anyone's advice; he'd also pawned a silver-gilt bowl worth eight marks. The food was awful, the prior didn't look after the monks if they were ill, and a woman called Isabel Warner was often there 'under suspicious circumstances'. The bishop adjourned the visitation to give them time to sort things out, and the prior was replaced the following year.

In 1514, the visitation showed that the canons weren't obedient and didn't attend services properly, the canons weren't looked after if they were ill, and Canon Ixning owed 55 shillings and 3 pence (a little over £1,200 in terms of today's money). Things were better in 1520, although one of the canons, George Walden, refused to turn up to the enquiry. In 1526, all was well apart from two of the novices thinking that one of the servants was insolent, and the other two notices complaining that they didn't have enough money to 'provide themselves with necessaries'.

1532 saw complaints about shoes – Canon Sharpyng and Canon Harvey admitting to having 'pointed shoes'. Other complains included lack of silence and the younger canons leaving the cloisters when they shouldn't. The bishop ordered that the canons should go to the dorter straight after compline and nobody was allowed to go out without the prior's permission – and the pointed shoes had to go, too.

There doesn't appear to be a record of a visit by Legh, Leyton or Ap Rice, but the king's commissioners said there were five priests and 'the name ys good as we can lerne by reporte of there neybures'. The house was suppressed in September 1536 and the property was leased to Sir Edmund Knevett of Buckenham Castle.

One further scandal was when John Tumour confessed to Richard Southwell that he'd heard that Hugh Wilkinson had offered John Lok an angel noble to kill the king's visitors in their beds at Buckenham Abbey. However, according to the nineteenth-century scholar Augustus Jessopp, it wasn't a plot: just a reflection of local discontent about the suppression of the monasteries.

The building of New Buckenham Castle

New Buckenham castle had an inner and two outer baileys with earth walls, and a stone gatehouse. The east bailey (known rather picturesquely as Knightriders Ward, according to an old document) is the earliest of the baileys and was reached through a gateway to the east. This gateway was destroyed in the thirteenth century, when the bank of the ringwork was enlarged; the second bailey, a gatehouse and a defensive enclosure were constructed at the same time.

According to Henry Harrod, at its peak the castle had a keep, two circular towers, an entrance tower, a barbican, embattled walls and a moat. Part of the gateway, the 40-foot-high earthwork bailey and the keep are all that's left. The keep is thought to be the oldest and largest Norman circular stone keep in England.

William Stronghand and the tongueless lion

William d'Albini II was in France on business for Adelize, the dowager Queen of England, when he heard new of a tournament held by the Queen of France at Paris. She said that anyone who could beat her champion, Raoul, Lord of Poitou, would have a noble prize from her. William couldn't resist the challenge, even though it was rumoured that the widowed Queen of France wanted to marry again and would choose her new husband from the champions.

He duly won the tournament, but refused the hand of the Queen of France, saying that he had already promised to marry Adelize, Henry I's widow. She summoned him to her garden, gave him jewels and promised to marry him if he would leave the service of Queen Adelize. She pointed out that if he married Adelize he wouldn't be king, but if he married the Queen of France he would have equal honours. William knelt at her feet, kissed her robe and explained that he couldn't be false to Adeliza – his hand, his love and his life were plighted to her.

The Queen of France flew into a jealous rage, but William refused to be cowed. She changed tactics, pretending to be nice and sweet, and asked him to walk with her in the garden because she wanted to show him something special.

'Something special' turned out to be a lion in a den at the bottom of the garden. As they walked in through the bars, William said he wasn't afraid, so the Queen of France told him to prove it – she ran back to the bars, and locked William in with the lion, expecting the beast to maul the Queen of England's champion.

William's response was to roll his cloak about his arm, put his hand into the lion's mouth, and (rather horribly) tear out its tongue. He sent it to the Queen of France – and from that day on he had the emblem of a tongueless lion on his shield and banner.

The Tateshale siege

By 1263, the castle was owened by the Tatsehale family. This might have been when the earthworks and banks in front of the castle gate were thrown up, because in that year the castle was under siege. Sir Robert Tateshale stood for the royal cause. Sir Robert's neighbours also supported the king, so they sent him supplies of men and arms, and gave him as much help as they could. Sir Robert de Mortimer sent a servant, Leonine, to the castle garrison with private information – and as a consequence they were able to defend the castle so that Sir Henry Hastings, an ally of Simon de Montfort, was forced to besiege the castle.

Sir Henry was furious and marched to de Mortimer's manors in the county, burning and destroying property as he went. The king defeated de Montfort, Buckenham remained intact, and Henry III stayed there often.

The second siege of Buckenham

There was a second siege in 1461. Sir John Knyvet had inherited the barony and the castle, but failed to pay £100 to the crown (the equivalent of just over £43,000 in today's money) on his inheritance, so the royal escheator was sent to sieze the castle.

He reported:

> On Tuesday before St Mathew last [i.e. 15 September – St Matthew's Day is 21 September and was on a Monday in 1461], we entered the outer Ward of the Castle to the foot of a bridge, called a 'draught brigge', across the water and found it raised so that we could not enter and Alice, the wife of John Knyvet, appeared in a little tower over the inner foot of the bridge, keeping the Castle with slings, paveises, faggots, timber and other armaments of war. 'Master Twyer,' she cried, 'ye be a justice of the pees and I require you to keep the pees for I wall not leve the possession of this castell to dye there fore, and if ye begyn to breake the pees or make any warre to get the place of me, I shall defend me, for liefer i had

in sych wyse to dye than to be slayne when my husband cometh home, for he chargeth me to keep it.'

Faced with shields, slings and the threat of burning timber being lobbed his way, the escheator decided that discretion was definitely the better part of valour – and retreated!

Never hit a servant...

In 1541 Sir Edmund Knyvet, the owner of Buckenham castle, was in severe trouble for striking Master Clere, one of the Earl of Surrey's servants, in the king's house. He was found guilty and sentenced to lose his right hand; he would also be left in prison and the king would seize his lands and goods.

There's some truly gruesome details in Howell's *State Trials* of who was to be there to carry out the sentence and why: the 'sergeant chirurgeon' with his instruments, the sergeant of the woodyard with the block, the master cook who'd 'set the knife on the right joint', the sergeant of the poultry (who would cut off the head of a cockerel on the same block and with the same knife), a woman from the 'chaundry' with a 'searing cloth' (presumably to staunch the blood), and a yeoman of the scullery with a pan of fire to heat the irons and a pan of water to cool them.

At the bar, Sir Edmund asked the king to take his left hand rather than his right, on the grounds that he was right-handed and would be able to do good service to the king with his right hand. The king considered this. He was told that Sir Edmund had a 'gentle heart', and there were good reports of him in the court, so Sir Edmund was pardoned and allowed to go free without losing a hand or his lands and money.

The end of the castle

The castle was defortified in the 1640s. The owner, Sir Philip Knyvet, demolished it in 1649 – possibly by order of parliament. He sold the estate to Hugh Audley (who later became the sheriff of Norfolk) for £18,508 and 10s (the equivalent to almost £1.7 million in today's money).

Secret tunnels

As often with castles, there is a myth regarding a secret tunnel. In the case of Buckenham Castle, it's that one leads to Old Buckenham Abbey, one leads to Boyland Hall (in Morningthorpe, demolished in 1947) and one leads to Kenninghall Place (the royal palace at Kenninghall; the remains are part of a farm). However, any tunnels that do exist are likely to be drainage tunnels rather than conspiratorial ones.

North Elmham Chapel

Remains of the chapel at North Elmham.

North Elmham chapel is located about 6 miles north of East Dereham on the B1110 (OS map reference TF 9893 2165). It's in the care of English Heritage and managed by North Elmham Parish Council, and is open to the public.

The chapel is the ruins of an early twelfth-century chapel built by Bishop Herbert de Losinga, and stands on the site of a pre-Conquest timber cathedral and cemetery. The chapel was incorporated into a fortified manor by Bishop Henry Despenser (the 'fighting bishop of Norwich') in 1388, when a moat was added as well as a curtain wall and outer bailey earthworks. It has been referred to as a 'cathedral' because there was originally a wooden cathedral here – but the see was removed to Thetford after the Conquest, and then from Thetford to Norwich, so the ruins are actually those of a private chapel rather than a Norman cathedral.

The bishop and the Rising of 1381

Although there are no ghosts attached as such to North Elmham, Bishop Despenser certainly put a few people to death in his time, and he was instrumental in suppressing the rising in Norfolk in 1381.

The causes of the revolt itself are complex – and the revolt included leaders of manorial communities as well as peasants, so it isn't just the 'peasants' revolt'. At the time the country was recovering from the impact of the Black Death, which had a death rate of around a third to half the population and led to incredible hardships among the poor. The church still insisted on collecting tithes, despite the fact that parishioners were starving. Just as villeins were starting to negotiate their freedom and the freemen were negotiating higher wages (some by moving to wherever the highest rates would be paid), the king passed the Statute of Labourers which decreed that there would be no wage rises for the freemen and no freedom for the villeins, and nobody was allowed to move away from their villages.

There were unpopular poll taxes from 1377 to 1381 to help pay for the war against France; the last one was a shilling per head, nearly a week's wages for the peasant, and the tax was the same for everyone regardless of income. Many people hid rather than paying taxes, but the king announced he would be sending out new tax collectors and those who had evaded the tax would be punished. The people started to rebel. Tax collectors were attacked, and property of the church and the nobility was destroyed. Led by Wat Tyler, the rebels burned tax records and marched to London to demand fair treatment from the king – in particular, fair wages, the end of market monopolies and an end to the feudal system.

Geoffrey Litester (or Lister), a dyer from Felmingham, helped to gather dissidents at Mousehold on June 11 – but the unrest in the county wasn't just about getting fair treatment for the peasants. The rebels invited Sir Robert Salle to join them – they hoped that because he wasn't born a noble, he might sympathise with their cause. When he refused, the crowd turned on him and killed him. Litester invaded the city, beheaded a JP, established himself at Norwich Castle (as 'King of the Commons') and then his men seized and publicly burned the deeds and court rolls of Carrow priory.

Carving of Bishop Despenser from a misericord in St Margaret's Church, King's Lynn.

Litester's men then turned on Yarmouth; they plundered the town, burned the town charters, and broke into the gaol – where they killed three of the four inmates just because they were Flemings.

When Wat Tyler was killed during a summit with Richard II at Smithfield on June 15, Litester decided to try and negotiate a settlement. He sent some of his men to London with the money he'd taken from Norwich and two hostage knights – but they met Henry Despenser just outside Newmarket. Despenser had heard the news of the rebellion and marched from his manor in Burleigh to deal with it. He gave the rebels absolution, then executed them: he cut off the heads of Litester's three men and displayed them on a pillory, then gathered his forces to fight Litester.

Although there were other risings – notably at St Benet's Abbey (see page 63), where the rebels hoped either to capture or talk to Despenser – Litester retreated to North Walsham, where he was defeated by Depenser. Several of his followers hid in the church, which was being built at the time – but Despenser knew that the building hadn't been consecrated, so he cut them to pieces inside the church.

Litester was tried, then hanged, drawn and quartered on 26 June; the quarters were displayed at Norwich, Great Yarmouth, King's Lynn and North Walsham to dissuade other potential rebels. The battle site was marked by three stone crosses, of which two remain on the Norwich Road at North Walsham.

The end of the chapel

The chapel became derelict in the sixteenth century and its stone was removed for use elsewhere.

Carrow Priory

Carrow Priory is the ruins of a Benedictine nunnery, located near the junction of King Street and Bracondale in Norwich (OS map reference TG 2425 0739). Although it's often referred to as 'Carrow Abbey', it never actually had the status of an abbey. The main surviving building is the Prioress's House, which was heavily altered in 1514. The site was bought by Colman's 1878 and J. J. Colman converted the building into a library for his collection. It's not open to the public.

The ruins of Carrow Priory, taken from the garden in the early twentieth century. Picture courtesy of Norfolk County Council Library and Information Service.

The beginnings of the priory

Two sisters, Seyna and Lescelina (whose name is shown in some documents as Leftelina), began building the priory in 1146, and it was dedicated to the honour of St Mary of Carhowe. It's thought that the priory was an offshoot of an older Benedictine nunnery in Norwich that was dedicated to St Mary and St John; King Stephen was the first to endow the foundation in 1146.

The priory was originally built for a prioress and nine Benedictine nuns. According to Pevsner, the church was 195 feet long and was the largest Norman ecclesiastic building in the city after the cathedral.

The last prioress, Isabel Wygun, built herself a large house of flint and brick, and her personal rebus of a Y and a gun is still visible in the fireplace.

The Rising of 1381

The priory was caught up in the Rising (aka the Peasants' Revolt); on 18 June 1381, Adam Smith and Henry Stanford of Wroxham forced the prioress to surrender her court rolls, which they burned.

Murder and sanctuary

In 1416, William Koc of Trowse was murdered – he was set upon by seven men and beaten to death with spades (including a 'molspade') and sticks. His widow, Margaret, went to the magistrates and accused Edith Wilton, the prioress, and Agnes Gerbald, one of the nuns, of harbouring his murderers in sanctuary at the priory. The magistrates arrested Edith and put her in prison, and Henry V called her to Westminster to plead her case. The court was adjourned several times, and in July 1416 Edith was acquitted on a technicality – because the events took place in the county of Norwich rather in than the county of Norfolk, which was specified on the legal documents.

Interestingly, Edith didn't claim benefit of clergy – the law at the time meant that clergymen could claim they were outside the jurisdiction of common law and could be tried by canon law (i.e. church law) instead. This is possibly because women weren't able to be ordained at the time and therefore, even though she was a nun, she wasn't strictly speaking a cleric, so she had to abide by common law rather than church law. Even more interestingly, William Cotesham, the ringleader of the attackers, was given a royal pardon.

This may have been a political case, because in 1416 Edith Wilton brought a case against the prior of Norwich Cathedral for driving her cattle off her land at Bracondale and extorting money – again, she said that the land was part of the county of Norwich rather than the county of Norfolk, so it was therefore outside the cathedral's jurisdiction. (This was a common argument in tensions between the citizens of Norwich and the Cathedral Priory.) The abbot was found in the wrong and had to pay £40.

In another case, Edith accused the prior and one of his monks (the same monk who'd been involved in the extortion case) of breaking into her land and destroying trees and fish.

Eventually, the rows between the cathedral priory and Carrow were settled in 1419.

Visitations

As with all religious establishments, the priory was seen regularly by the bishop in his 'visitations' – this was basically an appraisal of the management of the establishment, as the bishop would talk to the monks and nuns to check whether things were as they should be, i.e. that religious observances were being made, the buildings were in good condition, and accounts were done properly.

In 1492, the bishop discovered that Catharine Segryme, the prioress, confided more in 'a certain Margaret Knight, now absent' than in anyone else, and that bread was scarce. But in 1526 there was a much more interesting complaint – that on Christmas day they 'make the youngest nun pretend to be Lady Abbess' and she has to 'consume and waste all she has obtained by alms or the gifts of her friends' – a custom very similar to the Lord of Misrule. Richard Nix, the bishop, said that 'for the future the assuming of the character of abbess [should] be discontinued'; he also upheld two other complaints and ordered the nuns to get a clock and to observe the rule of silence.

In 1532, the complaints were relatively minor. Margaret Steward, the sub-prioress, said that some of the younger nuns wore silk waistbands and were addicted to gossip, while Joan Botulph said that the nuns didn't wear veils when they left the nunnery and the festival of relics wasn't observed. Matilda Gravell said that one of the nuns was meant to wait on the others at table, but it didn't happen. The injunctions were that the younger nuns should sit together in the afternoon, the subprioress should only let the nuns be absent from compline once a week, the feast of relics should be observed, and the prioress should make sure one of the nuns served her sisters at table.

Philip Sparrow

While he was Rector of Diss, probably around the period 1505-9, the poet John Skelton wrote the poem 'Philip Sparrow' about a pet bird, belonging to Jane Scrope, which was killed by a cat from Carrow Priory. The poem, in two parts, has been called a study in innocence and experience; the first part is in the voice of Jane, lamenting the loss of her sparrow, and the second is a treatise on Jane's beauty. It begins:

> *Pla ce bo!*
> Who is there, who?
> *Di le xi!*
> Dame Margery,
> *Fa, re, my, my.*
> Wherefore and why, why?
> For the soul of Philip Sparrow
> That was late slain at Carrow,
> Among the Nunnes Black.

Dissolution and after

At the dissolution, the site and revenues were granted in 1538 to Sir John Shelton (Anne Boleyn's uncle-in-law). The nineteenth-century painter and engraver John Sell Cotman mentioned a tradition that some of the materials from the abbey were used to build the hall at Arminghall. At one point, the prioress's house belonged to Roger Kerrison, a mayor of Norwich whose banking firm fell into debt and he was made bankrupt – particularly shocking to the citizens of Norwich because he also collected taxes for the Government, who were unable to recover the money Kerrison had collected.

J. J. Colman bought the house in 1878 and converted it to a library for his collection (which he left to the city). He was very friendly with Gladstone, the prime minister, who stayed there in May 1890 before addressing the city. The composer Elgar stayed there in October 1905 while visiting the Norwich Festival and described the house as 'beautiful and delightful'.

Tunnels and excavations

In common with many of the religious houses, Carrow Priory allegedly had a secret tunnel. W. B. Gerish (in his unpublished notes on Norfolk folklore from the early twentieth century) says that the tunnel led to Norwich castle – and that a pig once got lost in it! (Sadly, what happened to the pig isn't recorded.)

The nineteenth-century historian Walter Rye reported that a 'very old man,' Mr Wright, told him that the cow-keeper Edward Meek once lived in the kitchen part of the priory; when he pulled up the skirting under the window of the parlour, he found enough money to be able to hire a farm at Janwell. He repeated the story of the 'fat pig' getting lost in a tunnel, and also that a stone coffin was found standing up endways while men were digging for chalk in the area. When the priory was excavated in 1981, nine intact burials were found in the choir and side chapels, and two more just to the north of the church.

Norwich Castle

Norwich castle (off Castle Meadow, Norwich – OS map reference TG 23226 08457) dominates the skyline, with its Norman keep measuring 95 feet by 90 feet by 70 feet. It's the city museum and is open to the public.

The building of the castle

Historians disagree about when the first castle existed in Norwich. There may have been a castle on the site as early as 575, firstly as the residence of King Uffa and then of King Anna (the king of the Angles) in 642. If this was the case, it was probably destroyed when Sweyn sacked Norwich in 1004, and was possibly rebuilt by Cnut in 1017.

However, we do have more documentary evidence for what happened later in the eleventh century. The motte and bailey was built in around 1067 by William Fitz-Osbern, the earl of Hereford, and there was probably just a timber and earthwork fortification on the top – though the motte was apparently the largest in England. The castle was complete by 1075, when it withstood siege by Archbishop Lanfranc (see below). According to Pevsner, Norwich Castle was William I's only castle in Norfolk. The *Domesday Book* says that 98 properties were destroyed to make way for the earthworks; however, as around 200 houses in Norwich were empty and dilapidated at the time, it's likely that most of those 98 properties were in a poor condition to start with.

Why did William build such a visible symbol of his power in Norwich? Two of the likely reasons are that King Harold's brother had been the Earl of East Anglia

Norwich Castle.

Norwich Castle, plate from Thomas Kitson Cromwell's Excursions Through Norfolk, *Vol I, 1818.*

(so this showed William had conquered the earl), and also because William Fitz-Osbern (the joint viceroy in England with Bishop Odo of Bayeux, the Conquerer's half-brother) used Norwich as his eastern headquarters and it made sense for a defensive building to be there.

In around 1100, the motte was heightened and the ditch was deepened, and the square keep was built to serve as a royal palace. The bailey was also expanded in the twelfth century. By 1200, the castle fee stretched as far London Street and King Street; Castle Meadow, Farmer's Avenue and Cattle Market Street run along the edge of the original boundaries.

The castle as a gaol

The castle was used as a gaol from 1220. Additional buildings were constructed, but they gradually decayed until the castle was refortified during the Civil War. The prison buildings were demolished and rebuilt by Sir John Soane in 1789–93; there were more alterations in 1820, and was refaced in Bath stone (rather than the original Caen stone) by Anthony Salvin in 1834–9. Public executions took place in the castle ditches on Saturdays (as public entertainment, to the disgust of Charles Dickens), though after 1867 the authorities moved the hangings to Monday mornings in the hope of avoiding trouble among the crowds – drunkenness and pickpocketing were rife.

In 1887, after the new gaol opened on Plumstead Road/Britannia Road, the city bought the castle and converted it to a museum.

The siege of Norwich Castle

The castle was invested in 1075, and a constable was to hold the castle in the name of King William. The first constable of Norwich Castle was Ralph de Guader, the Earl of Norfolk and Suffolk. Ralph had been born in Norfolk to an English father (who was the staller or horse-master to Edward the Confessor) and a Breton mother. De Guader wasn't particularly popular in England because he was the only English earl to fight on William's side at the Battle of Hastings – outlawed by King Harold, he led a group of Bretons on the Norman side.

De Guader was very friendly with William Fitz-Osbern's son Roger – a man described by the Anglo-Saxon chroniclers as a 'hateful youth, full of perfidy'. When Fitz-Osbern was killed in Flanders, Roger inherited the earldom of Hereford and the English estates. And then de Guader decided to marry Emma, the earl of Hereford's sister – possibly a dynastic marriage (as Hereford was very powerful), but possibly also a love match because Emma stuck by him in the trouble that followed.

Hereford was already in trouble with William and in the year before the castle's investiture had received several letters from the regent, Archbishop Lanfranc, reminding him of his loyalty to the king. Eventually, Lanfranc lost patience with Hereford and excommunicated him, saying that he should submit to the king's mercy and make restitution to the king and to any other man he had wronged. Hereford did nothing of the kind, and in 1075 he permitted (and probably encouraged) Emma to marry his friend de Guader. William I refused flatly to sanction the marriage; it's likely that he realised how dangerous Hereford and de Guader were, and their combined forces could only spell trouble. De Guader ignored the fact that he didn't have the king's blessing and celebrated the marriage at Exning in Cambridgeshire with a huge party. Bearing in mind that the Earl of Hereford had been excommunicated, which meant that no religious official should have anything to do with him, it's surprising that the 'bride-ale' was attended by so many bishops and abbots, as well as de Guader's Breton friends. This was tantamount to defying the king – and it ended in tears.

As the *Anglo-Saxon Chronicle* put it:

Þær wes þæt bryd eala   mannum to beala
(There was that bride ale, which was many man's bale.)

Huge amounts of beer and wine were drunk. The guests started to complain about William and, according to the *Anglo-Saxon Chronicle*, took advice about 'how they might drive their lord out of the kingdom'. De Guader willingly agreed to help Hereford. Waltheof, the Earl of Northumberland, Northampton and Huntingdon, was also at the party. He was also a known rebel, as he'd joined a Danish attack on York only three years after submitting to William after the Battle of Hastings. Hereford and de Guader saw him as a natural part of their plot, despite the fact that Waltheof had married William's niece, Judith, and should have been firmly on William's side.

Hereford and de Guader's proposal was that they should drive William out of the country, then divide the country into three. One of them would rule as the king, and the other two would remain earls; each would have a third of the country.

The next morning, once Waltheof had sobered up (and possibly talked to his wife!), he thought better of it and confessed to Lanfranc. Lanfranc made him do penances for the church, then told Waltheof he had to go to Normandy and explain the situation to William. Waltheof went to France, laden with gifts, and asked William to forgive him. William appeared to do so, and kept Waltheof with him – under extremely close supervision.

Meanwhile, de Guader and Hereford rebelled openly. De Guader asked his family in Brittany and Denmark to help him. English Bretons came to his aid, and King Sweyn sent de Guader a fleet under the command of his son Cnut and Earl Hakon. Lanfranc moved swiftly to crush the rebellion and called the rest of England to his aid. According to the chronicler Simeon of Jarrow, Wulfstan, the bishop of Worcester, joined forces with Aethelwig, the abbot of Evesham. Together they prevented Hereford crossing over the Severn to join de Guader's forces. At the Severn, Odo of Bayeux, Geoffrey of Constance, Richard de Bienfait and William de Warenne cut off the right foot of every prisoner they made – meaning that they wouldn't ever be able to ride again, let alone fight against William.

Odo and Geoffrey went into battle against de Guader just outside Cambridge. Realising that his forces weren't strong enough to resist them, de Guader fled back to Norwich. Lanfranc reported to William that *Rodolfus traditur* (Ralph the traitor) and his army were fleeing, and the king's men were chasing him.

Hereford was captured and thrown into prison. Waltheof was also imprisoned; although he hadn't actually done anything rebellious and had told William every-thing he knew, William saw Waltheof as a danger to the country because he'd listened to traitors – particularly when he realised that Waltheof's old Danish comrades were in the vicinity. (Not that the Danes did much – according to the *Anglo-Saxon Chronicle*, the fleet of two hundred ships decided that it wasn't strong enough to fight William, so Cnut went to York and looted St Peter's Minster instead.)

De Guader entrusted the castle and a garrison into Emma's hands and fled to Brittany by ship; at the time, there was an estuary from Yarmouth meadows to Harford Bridges, so shipping links to Norwich were very good. From Brittany, de Guader travelled to Denmark, hoping for aid from the Danish side of his family.

Meanwhile, Odo and Geoffrey laid siege to Norwich Castle.

Emma would have had good cause to throw her lot in with William. Her grandfather had been William's guardian; her father had been William's best friend; and her family were connected to the dukes of Normandy. Her new husband had basically deserted her and left her to defend the castle as best as she could.

But Emma was a strong woman. Despite the no-show of the promised help from de Guader, or any Danish or Breton ships, she defended the castle with her garrison of Armorican Bretons. According to the nineteenth-century historian A. D. Bayne, the castle 'was much injured' during the siege. But Emma and her garrison held out for three months, until they were finally starved into surrender. Lanfranc was so impressed by her bravery that he negotiated a very fair settlement with her; rather than chopping off feet or hands, he gave her and her men forty days to leave the country forever.

William meanwhile followed de Guader to Brittany and besieged him in his castle at Dol. However, Alan Feargent, the Duke of Bretagne, and King Philip of France came to de Guader's aid and William had to give up. The *Anglo-Saxon Chronicle* notes that William lost 'men and horses and much treasure'; William also ended up negotiating a treaty that meant the Duke of Bretagne would marry William's daughter Constance.

Lanfranc wrote to William, saying that the realm was cleared from the 'infection' of 'Breton scum', adding that:

The landless mercenaries who served Ralph the traitor and his associates begged for and were granted the same terms within the limit of one month. Bishop Geoffrey, William of Warenne and Robert Malet have remained in the castle itself with 300 heavily armed soldiers, supported by a large force of slingers and siege engineers.

De Guader's rebellion was over. Emma, taking advantage of the terms she'd negotiated with Lanfranc, joined her husband in Brittany and they lived quietly for the next twenty years. When he went on the First Crusade in 1096, she went with him. De Guader died at some point between Nicaea and Jerusalem, and it's assumed that Emma died at the same time.

At the Midwinter Gemot or parliament on 25 December 1075, Hereford and Waltheof were brought to trial. De Guader was condemned in his absence. Hereford was imprisoned for life, fined heavily and his lands confiscated; his followers were punished by having their eyes put out or their hands cut off, some were banished, some were 'put to shame' and others hung in a gibbet.

Waltheof defended himself; his sentence was deferred and he was kept in prison in Winchester until the Pentecostal Gemot or parliament of 1076. Again he argued his case, but he was beheaded on 31 May and subsequently became a martyr, with signs and wonders seen at his tomb in Crowland.

As for Norwich's punishment – the *Domesday Book* says that thirty-two burgesses fled the town and others were ruined by confiscation of their property. The yearly 'farm' (the lease of the revenues from tolls and court fines) that the burgesses had to pay to the king was tripled to £90 (the equivalent of around £50,000 in modern terms). After Christmas at Westminster, William decided to punish everyone in Norwich who'd attended de Guader's wedding – some had their eyes put out, some were banished, and some had to forfeit all their possessions.

More sieges

According to the eighteenth-century historian Francis Blomefield, Roger Bigod, who'd succeeded Ralph de Guader as the earl of Norfolk, seized the castle in 1088 and garrisoned it to help Robert Curthose, the Duke of Normandy, against William Rufus. Peace came in 1091, and Roger continued to hold the castle.

In 1136, during the civil war between Stephen and Matilda, it was rumoured that Stephen had been killed. Hugh Bigod, the earl of Norfolk (son of Roger Bigod, above), seized Norwich castle and refused to hand it over to anyone other than the king.

In 1172, Hugh Bigod supported the rebellion of Henry II's son; in return, he was offered the constableship of Norwich Castle. In July 1174 his soldiers, together with Flemish mercenaries, captured Norwich castle; however, at the end of July Hugh was forced to submit to Henry II, who fined him heavily and demolished his castle at Framlingham. Hugh died on a pilgrimage to Jerusalem in 1177 and he was buried at Thetford Priory.

Hugh's son Roger was among the dissident barons against King John, and John seized the castle. After John died in 1216, Louis Dauphin (the heir of the King of France) seized the castle and held it under siege, but the following year he was paid off and left the country.

Spooks

It's surprising that, given that the castle was used as a gaol and the number of people executed there over the years, that more ghosts haven't been reported.

In 1820, several prisoners claimed to be scared 'half to death' by something indescribable – a ghost. This may have been the ghost who's been seen in modern times, a lady dressed in black early-Victorian clothes. Allegedly, she wanders around the art exhibition area of the museum – which was once part of the gaol buildings – then turns a corner and vanishes. It's thought that the old lady might be Martha Alden, one of the few women hanged at the castle for cutting off her husband's head with a billhook. (In her defence, she was a battered wife and he'd drunk away all her inheritance – as well as threatening to murder her.)

I've also come across a reference that the ghost of Robert Kett, leader of the rebels in 1549, has been seen at the castle (see Wymondham Abbey, page 154, for details of the rebellion). Kett was hung alive in chains from the walls of the castle, and allegedly his ghost has been seen rotting in its swinging cage.

A grave with a hoard of silver and gold

The early twentieth-century folkorist, W. B. Gerish, has a story that the original castle was build before Roman times by a king galled Gurgunt (or possibly Gungunt or Gungant). When he died, a huge mound was raised for him (i.e. the one we see in Norwich today) and he sits there still, next to a huge table piled with a hoard of silver and gold, with his sword in his hand.

Tunnels

Most castles have legendary secret tunnels, and Norwich castle is no exception.

The first is meant to lead from the castle to the Guildhall – and indeed there are fourteenth-century vaults beneath the Guildhall. The second leads to Carrow Priory (see page 96). A third leads to the cathedral (see page 103), and according to W. B. Gerish another led to the Crown Derby pub near the Guildhall. (However in 1914, when Gerish was writing, no pub in the area was called the Crown Derby. The nearest pub to the Guildhall was the Guildhall Stores at 2, Market Place.)

One tunnel that definitely exists is the one built in the 1830s, which the prisoners used to go from the prison to the courts in the Shire Hall. Nowadays the tunnel us used for visitors to the castle to visit the regimental museum, and part of it has been made into a display of a reconstructed WWI communication trench.

The Cathedral Priory of the Holy Trinity, Norwich

Norwich cathedral, viewed from the cloisters.

The Cathedral Priory of the Holy Trinity was attached to the Cathedral in the Close, Norwich (OS map reference TG 235 089), and was a house of Benedictine monks. The visible remains of the priory include the cloisters (which are the largest surviving monastic cloisters in England), the hostry, and stone remains of six piers with water holding bases belonging to the south façade of the Infirmary Hall.

The beginnings of the cathedral and the priory

The cathedral was built by Herbert de Losinga, allegedly as penance for committing the sin of simony – i.e. buying his own appointment as the bishop of East Anglia and his father's appointment as the abbot of Winchester. De Losinga paid the king £1,900 (the equivalent of nearly a million pounds in modern money) for his own appointment and half as much again for his father's appointment – but it's worth remembering that the king expected gifts when he appointed a bishop, and William Rufus had been very unhappy when Bishop Anselm only offered him £500. Evidently he was rather happier with de Losinga's gifts.

The foundation stone of the cathedral was laid in 1096, and work progressed fast enough for the monks to be able to inhabit some of the monastic buildings a mere five years later. When it was completed, the cathedral was the largest building in East Anglia, at 141m long and 54m wide (including the transepts).

Remains of the infirmary hall at Norwich Cathedral priory.

The riot of 1272

There had always been tensions between the citizens of Norwich and the monks; apart from the fact that building the cathedral meant the demolition of one of the city's original parish churches (St Michael's in Tombland – which was the richest church in the city at Domesday) and several homes, there were disputes over taxation rights and the areas which the priory and city charters covered. The monks claimed that the city charter didn't cover Tombland, Holmstreet (Bishopgate) or Spitelond (an area within the precincts of St Paul's Hospital, next to Cowgate), whereas the citizens felt that their charter covered the whole city. Henry III had to adjudicate several times, and each time he decided in favour of the priory.

It came to a head at the Trinity Fair in June 1272. The citizens set up a quintain for practising jousting and also various stalls in Tombland – but William Burnham, the prior, said the citizens were trespassing on priory property and ordered his servants to disperse everyone. The citizens weren't happy and drove the servants back to the priory – but then William le Messer shot a bolt from inside the priory and killed Adam de Newenton, one of the citizens. The city coroners held an inquest and arrested two priory servants for murder; in response, Burnham excommunicated the citizens.

A three-day riot followed on August 9. There are several accounts of the pro-ceedings, none of them neutral; unsurprisingly. the monastic chroniclers claimed that the citizens were at fault, and the city's chroniclers claimed that the monks were at fault.

The prior brought three bargeloads of armed men from Yarmouth, Norwich's traditional 'rival' of the time (probably from the priory at Yarmouth, which was a cell of the Norwich priory), and they marched through the city, beating drums and sounding trumpets. That night, a mob came from the priory; they killed and wounded several citizens and stole £20 (the equivalent of over £6,000 in terms of today's money) from the city merchant Alfred Cutler. Then they broke into Hugh de Bromholm's tavern and drank all they could, before emptying the casks on the floor to waste the remainder. They also allegedly burned down three houses belonging to citizens near Greyfriars.

The citizens wrote to the king to complain about the prior's actions – but they didn't wait for a reply. On 9 August, they gathered in the market place at Tombland to bring justice to the monks for making 'an illegal castle' in the city. Most sources say that around 120 citizens gathered in front of the priory gates, though the monastic chroniclers John of Oxnead and Bartholomew de Cotton claim it was more like 32,000. (This is unlikely, as the population of Norwich was estimated at 8,500 in the sixteenth century and was definitely smaller than that in the thirteenth century!)

The citizens burned down the Ethelbert gate to gain entrance to the priory. Then they burned the parish church of St Ethelbert and allegedly stole its books, ornaments and images. The next thing to catch fire was the bell-tower next to the church, which stood between the Ethelbert gate and the Erpingham gate. Who actually burned it down is less clear. Bartholomew Cotton claims that the citizens did it deliberately, by throwing fire from slings at the top of St George's church in Tombland. The *Liber de Antiquis Legibus* (the Corporation of London's 'Book of Ancient Laws', which chronicles various events in the country's history during the thirteenth century) gives the citizens' version of what happened and says that the priory smiths accidentally set fire to the bell-tower as they fled.

What happened next was a scene of great confusion. As for the damage done – that varies according to the sources. According to the monks, everything was burned down. The Pope's Bull claims that the Cathedral, belfry, dormitory, refectory, infirmary, treasury, sacristy, guest chamber and the whole place was burned down 'except three or four buildings'. Holinshed takes it even further, claiming that 'nothing was preserved except one little chapel'. However, that's clearly an exaggeration as the Cathedral is still standing, and its stonework was relatively unharmed – there are small traces of fire in the southern part of the choir and its pillars, but experts think that these may be due to a fire at the Cathedral a hundred years before the riot. John Causton, one of the monks, saved the cellar of the infirmary and the vaults by 'quenching the fire with the drink in them'.

Cotton claims that 'many monks, some subdeacons and some clerks' were killed – though only thirteen people defending the priory were recorded being killed, and none of them were monks. The monks fled and the citizens took books, gold, silver and vestments from the cathedral. We don't know where the monks gathered together again but they did make a stand, the day after the fire, because the records state that the prior killed John Casmus by hitting him on the head with a falchion (a broad, curved sword). The king's letters patent refer to 'conflagrations, homicides and losses... in the town' as well as in the priory, recognising that the monks had at least a share of the blame in the riot.

In the middle of August, Henry III sent three of his advisers to the city and ordered the sheriffs and burgesses of Norwich to help his men, and the following month he came to Norwich to see the situation for himself. Clearly he saw faults on both sides, as he placed the citizens under the wardenship of Hugh Pecche and Hervey de Stanhou, and the priory and its possessions under the wardenship of Robert de Waucham, Prior of Dunham.

Following the trial, thirty-four citizens were dragged about the streets by horses to the gallows, where they were hanged and their bodies burned; others were hanged, drawn and quartered, and the woman who was accused of setting fire to the gates was burned.

After Henry III's death on 16 November, Edward I confirmed the appointment of the wardens, and ordered an investigation. The jury decided that the church was burned by accident by the priory smiths, the prior had tried to burn the whole city and set fire to it in three places, and the prior was guilty of murder and robbery. Prior de Burnham was taken into custody to be tried by the bishop, who let him 'purge himself after the manner of ecclesiastics' – Burnham died soon afterwards, possibly from guilt or even from fury that he'd lost everything.

This sparked a diplomatic incident; Roger de Skerning, the bishop of Norwich, asked Pope Gregory to step in. The Pope said that the city's magistrates and bailiffs were to blame, and excommunicated the whole city. This meant everyone in Norwich should be 'strictly denounced and avoided by all men, and incapable of absolution'. Their bodies weren't allowed to be buried in any ecclesiastical cemetery, and if they'd already been buried they should be dug up again 'and cast out far away from Christian sepulture'. They would also be deprived of any benefices or fees, and their heirs 'to the fourth generation' were not allowed to be clerks or 'attain to any honour in any religious house' unless they had a special dispensation.

The priory demanded 4,000 marks for damage, but the pope referred it to the king. Edward's judgement was that the monks and citizens had to agree to be friends and send delegates to Rome to prove it to the pope. He also said that the city had to pay the Prior 500 marks a year for six years (a mark was a monetary unit which only existed on paper; it was measured at 2/3 of one pound sterling, or 13 shillings and four pence – so this was a total of 3,000 marks or £2,000, the equivalent of over £630,000 in terms of today's money). The city also had to give the priory a gold pyx weighing ten pounds and worth £100 (or £31,500 in terms of today's money) and make new gates for the priory. In return, the bishop lifted the excommunication in December and the Pope gave Norwich a General Absolution in 1276.

Building resumed at the cathedral; the citizens built the Ethelbert Gate in 1307, as requested, and then new cloisters were built, though they weren't completed until 1450 – partly because the Black Death killed much of the workforce in 1349-50.

Gladman's Insurrection, 1443

There was another riot in January 1443, known as Gladman's Insurrection. The row started over rights to grain mills (as usual between the city and the priory). The abbot of St Benet's claimed that the city's new mills on the Wensum interfered with the mills on his manor; the city agreed to let the Duke of Suffolk arbitrate. Suffolk sided with the priory and said the city's mills had to be taken down, and the city had to enter into various bonds to ensure they abided by all decisions. Clearly this was going to cause the city's bakers problems, and there was the real possibility of grain and bread shortages.

William Hempstede, the Mayor of Norwich, didn't want to enter into such a detrimental agreement. Allegedly, he declared that the city could kill the bishop and prior of Norwich as well as the abbot of St Benet's (see page 64) and spoil their goods. He also said that because the city was a county by itself, the king wouldn't be able to do anything about it.

John Gladman, one of the city's merchants, rode to the priory gates, wearing a paper crown and carrying a sceptre and sword; 3,000 men followed him, and they threatened to burn the priory and kill the prior and monks. They dug a tunnel under the gates, then stacked wood around them so they could burn the priory more easily. The priory gave them 'evidence, sealed with the seal of the city' (i.e. a list of priory privileges that the citizens wanted abolished). The citizens took the paper away, and kept the city gates shut against the king and his commissioners.

It seems that John Heydon was involved (see Baconsthorpe Castle, page 6). He had been the recorder of Norwich, and well paid for it – but he was very friendly with the prior and gave the prior information that could be used to win cases in court against the city. The mayor discovered this and promptly sacked Heydon (entirely reasonably!); Heydon bore a grudge against the mayor, and testified against him over Gladman's insurrection. Hempsteade was thrown into prison, and Thomas Wetherby (a former mayor who led the opposing faction in the city, and was friendly with Heydon and the Duke of Suffolk) took over government and used the city seal to ratify the Duke of Suffolk's judgement, before wrecking the city's mills.

An an inquest, the city's defence claimed that Gladman was simply crowned as 'Kyng of Cresemesse' (i.e. Lord of Misrule – apparently this was his usual role) and it was a Shrovetide 'sporting'. However, as the riot took place six weeks before the usual Shrovetide mummery was due, it's hardly a reasonable excuse. Why would Gladman dress up in his robes, followed by 'Lenten, clad in white with red herrings's skins, and his horse decked with oyster shells', when it was too early for the annual pageantry? One possibility is that it was allegorical, showing the time of plenty (Christmas) followed by the time of fasting (Lent – which would be made harder with the city mills being out of action); also, the oyster shells represented sadness and absence of mirth.

The result paralleled the riot of 1272 in that the city was excommunicated for a time, its liberties were aized by the king and they had to pay a fine – originally of £2,000 but it was eventually reduced to 1,000 marks (£666, 12s and 8d, or the equivalent of over £300,000 in today's money). Once the fine had been paid, the city's liberties were restored; and Wetherby's use of the city seal was declared illegal as the mayor was in prison at the time. Things settled down again after that, although every so often the arguments about rights over fairs and tolls blew up again.

Scandals

Given that there were on average around 45 monks in the priory, it's hardly surprising that discipline could sometimes be an issue. At the earliest visitation, that of Bishop John Salmon in 1308, all was well but the monks used pressure of work to evade divine service; Salmon said that at least two-thirds of the monks should attend services and all the monks (except those who were ill or in certain offices) should attend on days of festival. Around 40 years later, the visitation of William Bateman focused on lack of annual accounts and the fact the monks spent too much time dining out in the city with friends and eating meat.

In Bishop Goldwell's visitation of 1492, there were complaints that women (specifically the wives of the barber and the tailor) spent the night within the close, even though they were specifically forbidden in the precincts; valuables had been sold; and the sacrist 'dealt prodigally with his funds' and went out of the monastery at night. Silence wasn't properly observed the in choir, cloister, and dormitory; the monks sat and walked within the church and its enclosures, and spent too much time talking to 'women of doubtful character'. Laymen were allowed in the refectory, and the gates weren't shut regularly at night time so anyone could come in and out as they pleased. Specifically singled out was Father Dennis – not only did he hold too many offices (commoner, almoner, infirmarer, and pittancer), but he used one of the gardens, planted with saffron, for his own purposes.

By the next visitation, things had improved; but the visitation of 1514 showed that Robert Catton, the prior, had really let discipline slip – he didn't even turn up to the visitation! The sub-prior was 'profligate', the buildings were dilapidated, the monastery was in debt, and there was no regular schoolmaster. The number of the monks had fallen to thirty-five, and of those quite a few were unchaste, didn't wear the right habits and danced in the guest hall at night. Women came in and out of the monastery whenever they liked, the services were conducted in a slovenly manner, and sheep grazed in the cloister garth (i.e. yard or garden). The bishop gave the usual instructions and injunctions, and gave them six months in which to reform themselves.

By 1520 all was back to how it should be; the subprior and two of the most troublesome monks (John Sibyls and William Wingfield) had gone, and much of the trouble had gone with them. The only complaint was again about the sheep, and the bishop banned them from grazing in the cloister.

However, things were messy again by the time of the next visitation six years later. There were clearly factions within the priory. Two monks in particular were complained about: Thomas Sall and John Sall. Thomas was the third prior – but the subprior didn't like him and if Thomas imposed any penances on the junior monks, the subprior would let them off. This clearly wasn't good for priory discipline; and it was mentioned that the junior monks spent their time playing cards and backgammon, while the senior monks wore gaudy hats with satin rosettes and lappets (i.e. they were still too secular in their outlook). There were also complaints that the tailor's wife was 'familiar' towards Dr Rugge (who later became the prior of St Benet's) in public.

John Sall seemed to be quite a character – and also disliked. He was the priory communiarius, i.e. its chief accountant, and his own room for work; however, he wasn't supposed to sleep there, so he was pulled up for that. Also, he liked really fine clothes. Some of the complaints seem ridiculous now, nearly 500 years later – but they were duly made. His shoes had been seen tied with red bows, he wore dancing pumps, and he'd actually lifted his robes six inches to show his shoes to the juniors. In the end, it turned out that John's accounting wasn't as good as it should have been, so the bishop ordered him to give up the office of communiarius; the other charges didn't stick or were ignored.

At the last visitation in 1532, William Castleton was the prior. It seemed that he'd given up trying to keep the peace in the priory, as there were many quarrels among the monks, along with accusations of idleness and being 'dressy'. Someone complained that John Sall had appropriated a particularly fine silk cushion, and there were hints that Thomas Sall practised 'curious arts' (but see Walsingham Priory on page 141– it's possible that this was a legitimate chemical laboratory rather than an alchemical one).

Dissolution

The priory was dissolved on 2 May 1538, and was the first cathedral priory in the country to be dissolved. It was refounded immediately as a secular cathedral, with a dean and chapter instead of a prior and monks. The last prior, William Castleton, became the first dean of the cathedral. Of the 31 monks, some became part of the 8 required singing men of the cathedral, and some became parish priests. Many of the priory buildings were either destroyed or reused as part of the secular cathedral – the prior's house, for example, became the deanery. Incredible as it seems now to modern eyes, the infirmary block was demolished in 1806 to improve the view from the deanery.

Spooks

Naturally, there are spooky stories associated with the cathedral. One is that Cromwell, hearing that a group of Royalists were at the Maid's Head hotel, sent

his forces to Norwich in 1644 to capture them. As his henchmen went into the hotel, the Royalists retreated down a secret tunnel and stretched steel ropes across it. Cromwell's men and horses followed but, horribly, were beheaded by the steel ropes... and according to 'Ghostly Dave' Chisnell their ghostly hoofbeats can be heard under the ground around the area of the cathedral close at midnight near the end of January.

Engraving of the Infirmary from Norwich Cathedral priory, taken from Henry Harrod's Castles and Convents of Norfolk, 1857.

The cathedral has also been used for the setting of ghostly tales for film and television. M. R. James's ghost story 'The Stalls of Barchester Cathedral' was filmed here in 1971, and in late 2007 'My Talks with Dean Spanley' (release date 2008) was filmed here – a tale of canine reincarnation based on the book by Lord Dunsany and starring Peter O'Toole, Sam Neill and Jeremy Northam.

Tunnels

As with many of the religious institutions in the county, there are legendary tunnels leading from the cathedral. One apparently runs to the ruins of St Benet's Abbey, nine miles away; and another leads just across the road to the Samson and Hercules building in Tombland. The undercroft of a former house on the site, dating from the fifteenth century, is incorporated into the house, so there may be some truth to the rumour. The original figures of Samson and Hercules were made of wood, but were replaced by plaster images when Samson lost an arm. There's a legend that when the cathedral clock strikes 12, the statues step down from their pedestals (though why they come to life, what they do and when they return isn't recorded).

The cult of St William

One story that encompasses a scandal, a siege and spooky happenings is the tale of St William of Norwich. It's probably one of the most horrible tales ever to come out of the city, and it's very much bound up with the cathedral. The story was written up by one of the monks, Thomas of Monmouth, some years after the event, and it was embellished even more by William Capgrave in 1492.

So the story goes, William was born to a farmer and his wife about 1132. His mother dreamed of a fish with 12 red fins taken to heaven, and her father, a priest, interpreted the dream as meaning that she would have a son who would become famous at the age of twelve by the 'favour of the Holy Spirit'.

At the age of eight, William became apprentice to a skinner in Norwich and became friendly with the Jewish community. When he was twelve, he was 'enticed away' by the Jews, and was never seen alive again. A day or so later locals saw a light in the sky, and two of them ventured out to discover the body. The locals decided that the boy had been murdered by the Jews (even though there

was no evidence who had murdered him) and William's uncle demanded satisfaction through trial by ordeal.

The sheriff realised there was going to be trouble, so he took the Jews under his protection in the castle precincts (despite the fact that he owed them money and would profit by them being thrown out of the city – the sheriff's behaviour is about the only honourable bit in the story). The prior of Lewes, who'd been at the Synod in the city, saw the possibilities of profiting from making the boy a saint and asked for the body. The bishop of Norwich refused, and had the body moved; when it was washed, everyone smelled the 'odour of sanctity'. This was one of the signs of sainthood in the Middle Ages, along with a body not corrupting after death – which apparently also applied to William's case.

Detail of painted screen in Loddon Church showing the martydom of St William.

Thomas of Monmouth claimed that Theobald, a converted Jew from Cambridge, said that it was the custom for Jews to sacrifice a boy at Passover and he knew that Norwich had been chosen by lot as the place for the sacrifice that year. This was the first 'blood accusation' or 'blood libel' myth against the Jews in England; it was also repeated regarding Hugh of Lincoln in 1255. It was completely untrue, but the mud stuck.

The bishop of Norwich retired in 1146 and the sheriff died a couple of days later. Then Eleazar the Jew was murdered in 1148 (probably by Sir Simon de Noyers, a tenant of the priory who happened to owe Eleazar a lot of money), and the new bishop of Norwich said that as the Jews had murdered William first, that case had to sorted out before Eleazar's murder could be investigated. In the end, King Stephen had to come to Norwich to arbitrate; he postponed the case indefinitely.

And then the miracles started happening. A rose tree blossomed on William's grave until nearly Christmas; Botilda the cook's wife was having a difficult labour until she drank water which had had a fern from William's grave steeped in it, when she safely gave birth to a a son; and a girl from Dunwich prayed at the grave and was freed from the attentions of a fairy who kept offering to marry her. After that, there was a man 'vexed by an unclean spirit' who was tied up all night beside William's tomb and then slept and was cured on waking; a crippled boy was brought to the tomb by his father and walked away three days later.

The most amazing 'miracle' is that of a woman called Wimarc. Her husband had been taken by pirates, and she became a hostage in his stead. After much suffering, she and three other female prisoners decided to poison their jailer and put poison from a toad in his beer. He was suspicious and made them drink it first; the other women died, and Wimarc was at the point of death with grossly swollen limbs. The doctors she saw couldn't help her, so she visited several shrines, ending up at William's tomb. She knelt down, said a prayer, kissed the stone – then threw up. Apparently 'there was enough of it to fill a vessel of the largest size' and the stench was so bad that the whole congregation left the cathedral – the poor sacrists had to clean up and put herbs everywhere!

William's uncle Godwin Sturt had been profiting from the boy's death – he sold 'medicine' made from holy water in which he'd dipped the gag found in William's mouth. One woman said she needed the medicine but couldn't afford it; he said that if it was free she wouldn't value it, so she should get him a chicken. The woman asked St William to reward his uncle… and the next day, she was healed, while all the chickens belonging to Godwin had died – a nice piece of poetic justice.

The cult of St William had practically died out by the middle of the fourteenth century.

Norwich Priory of Whitefriars

Fourteenth-century stone arch: remains of the Whitefriars priory in Norwich.

Whitefriars Priory is the remains of a thirteenth-century Carmelite priory. The remaining arch is on Whitefriars in Norwich – OS map grid reference TG 23432 09200.

The beginnings of the priory

The priory was founded by Philip de Cougate (or Cowgate) in 1256. According to John Bale (who joined the order at Norwich at the very young age of 12 and was prior at Ipswich,) Philip de Cougate joined the priory after the death of his wife as a lay brother; Philip died on 23 April (Bale didn't give a year) and was buried in the priory. Bale also described the priory's library as 'the most beautiful in the order'.

The runaway monk

In about 1420, John Hawteyn was imprisoned at Whitefriars for six months, after running away from Maldon Priory and being brought back there by his family. Years later he said that he had been accepted under age (though he was asking for dispensation for his vows at time). *Apostasia a religione* (apostasy) occurred where a professed religious person abandoned the religious life and returned to the world; under church law and the laws of each religious order, it was a crime. Usually the runaways were arrested and excommunicated (which meant that nobody was allowed to have anything to do with you and you couldn't be buried in consecrated ground), although there are several recorded cases of apostates being pardoned and returning to the religious life. The religious orders weren't supposed to accept female novices under the age of 12 or male novices under the age of 14 (the same ages as for marriage), followed by a year's probation, but often the rules were bent.

The riot of 1452

According to the Paston letters, on 6 April 1452 a mob of about 40 men rode to Norwich on Maundy Thursday, 'jakked and salletted' (i.e. armoured), with bows and arrows, bullys and gloves. The following day, when the service was due, they came to the priory saying they wanted to hear evensong. They were told that the service wouldn't be held there or anywhere else in Norwich at that time of day – and they turned nasty, threatening to break down the doors of the priory. They said that they 'should have some men out of the place, quick (i.e. alive) or dead'. However, the citizens were firmly on the side of the priory, and the mayor and aldermen turned up with a 'great multitude of people'. The mayor threatened to arrest the rioters, who promptly left – much to the relief of the priory.

Scandals

Lady Eleanor Butler, daughter of the Earl of Shrewsbury, died on 30 June 1468 and was buried in the priory in July. She was part of a national scandal in 1483 when Richard, Duke of Gloucester claimed that Eleanor had a precontract of marriage with Edward IV before he married Elizabeth Woodville in May 1464, so Edward's children were illegitimate and therefore parliament should depose Edward V in favour of Richard.

But did Eleanor actually marry the king?

After the death of Eleanor's husband Sir Thomas Butler death in 1461, her father-in-law took back two of the estates he'd settled on them as a marriage gift – but he didn't have a licence to transfer the property and Edward IV seized them. Eleanor asked the king for the return of her properties and – being a notorious womaniser – he asked her to sleep with him. He promised to marry her, although there is no evidence of a betrothal or a marriage – at the time, the contract of marriage simply meant that Eleanor would have said the words 'I do marry you' to Edward (witnesses and a priest weren't necessary) followed by sexual intercourse.

Eleanor clearly wasn't around to testify as to whether or not she was betrothed to Edward or married him. Tudor historians said that the priest who claimed to have married them – Robert Stillington, the Bishop of Bath and Wells – had actually married Edward and Elizabeth Lucy (aka Elizabeth Waite), the mother of his illegitimate son Arthur Plantagenet.

However Edward's marriage to Elizabeth Woodville was clandestine, with no banns called and none of the king's ministers present – this was a way of avoiding problems in a marriage where an impediment existed. (It could also have been because he wanted to avoid criticism from his advisers, who wanted him to marry a French princess.) Richard said the impediment to Edward's marriage was the fact that he was already married to Eleanor. It was an adulterous relationship and therefore under church law at the time Edward couldn't have married Elizabeth, even after Eleanor's death, unless Elizabeth could prove that she hadn't known of his marriage to Eleanor. But because Edward married Elizabeth in a private house, in secret, canon law came down on the side of Richard – and he became King Richard III.

Dissolution and fraud

In 1538, the prior wrote to the Duke of Norfolk, asking him to take the surrender of their house as they were in distress. A few days later, John Pratt, the servant of Ralph Salter of Harpley, came to the priory when the prior was eating dinner, saying that he had a commission from the Lord Privy Seal to suppress the house. The prior was suspicious and asked him to produce the commission; he couldn't, so the prior took him to the mayoralty court, accusing him of being a cheat and an impostor. In court, Pratt admitted that he was trying to extort money; his idea was to frighten the prior into giving him an amount of money, either 40 shillings or £4 (worth around £820 and £1640 respectively in terms of today's money). On 19 October, the court ordered that Pratt should be carried round the market, with a 'bason' rung before him, and a paper on his head saying, 'for false feyning to be the kynge's commyssioner'. After this, rather horribly, his ears were nailed to the pillory and then cut off.

Meanwhile, the house was dissolved, and in 1542 the site was granted to Richard Andrews and Leonard Chamberlain.

Pentney Priory

P entney Priory is the remains of a fourteenth-century gatehouse belonging to a twelfth-century Augustian priory. It lies on Abbey Road in Pentney (OS map reference TF 7007 1209).

The beginnings of the priory

The priory was founded at some time before 1135 by Robert de Vaux. It was dedicated in honour of the Holy Trinity, the Blessed Virgin, and St Mary Magdalen. There were around 15-20 canons from the Augustinian order. Unusually, the original endowments included two salt pans – one at King's Lynn and one at South Wootton.

Gatehouse remains at Pentney.

Becket and Henry II

Pentney played a part in the struggle between Becket and Henry II. In around 1166, Hugh Bigod, the Earl of Norfolk, seized the priory's lands on a trumped-up recovery action against William de Vaux, the son of the founder. The priory appealed to Rome, and the pope ordered Becket to excommunicate the Earl.

This put Becket in a difficult position. If he excommunicated the Earl, it would upset the king; but if he didn't excommunicate the Earl, it would upset the pope. He tried opening negotiations between the Earl and the priory; apparently other lands were offered to the priory, but they refused because their site had been dedicated to God's service and they felt it was wrong to be used for secular purposes. The earl, meanwhile, refused to give the lands back to the priory.

Again, the pope ordered Becket to excommunicate the Earl of Norfolk – and also to excommunicate William de Vaux. Becket had to obey and told the bishops of Norwich and Ely to publish the order, and meanwhile told to canons not to make any rash compromises. Quite what happened next was unclear, but the priory lands remained with the canons and the Earl of Norfolk was eventually absolved by the pope. And Becket meanwhile continued to clash with the king.

Visitations

Pentney had an outstanding reputation for good work in the community, and in the visitation of 1492 it was said to be the most efficient in the county – the buildings were in good repair, and the school and divine services were well attended. In 1514, there was a complaint that they had no schoolmaster and the prior hadn't given any accounts for two years; but everyone else reported *'omnia bene'* and no injunctions were issued. The visitations of 1520, 1526 and 1532 were equally blameless, except for the house needing repairs in 1532.

Scandals and dissolution

Thomas Legh and John Ap Rice, as usual, visited the priory to make a report in 1536. According to them, Robert Codde, the prior, admitted that he'd had 'criminal conversation' (i.e. sex) with the abbess of Marham (see page 83). Five of the canons also claimed that they were incontinent (in other words, they didn't keep their vow of celibacy). However, this is very unlikely to be true, as the county commissioners made a completely different report: 'alle Prystes of very honest name and goode religious persones who doue desyre the kynges highness to contynue and remayne in religione' – and after the dissolution the prior was given a pension of £24. Sir Richard Southwell, the king's commissioner, actually wrote to Cromwell in May 1536 saying that Pentney shouldn't be suppressed because the canons did so much good among the poor:

> We beseech your favour for the Prior of Pentney, assuring you that he relieves those quarters wonderously where he dwells and it would be a pity not to spare a house that feeds so many poor, which is in good state of repair, maintains good services and does so many charitable deeds.

There was clearly some fear that suppressing the priory would upset the locals, and in October 1536 the order came to leave the priory alone 'because of insurrection in the north parts'. However, it was finally suppressed in February 1537, and the prior was appointed as the master of St Giles' hospital in Norwich. The priory and its lands were granted to Thomas, the Earl of Rutland, in February 1538.

The priory finally fell into ruin during the Civil War, when Cromwell's men sailed up the River Nar and used the buildings for target practice. The stone was then used as building material in the village (which, at the time of writing, is under threat of being ruined by a quarry).

Shouldham Priory

The only remains of Shouldham Priory are earthworks (enclosures, water channels and fishponds) to the south of Abbey Farm on Warren Road, which was built over the nave of the priory church and uses some of the ashlar stone in its buildings (OS map reference TF 6810 0947). The site isn't open to the public.

The beginnings of the priory

The priory was founded in about 1190 by Geoffrey FitzPiers, earl of Essex, for Gilbertine canons and nuns. It was dedicated to the Holy Cross and the Blessed Virgin. FitzPiers died in 1212.

Clashes and assaults

Richard Maillie complained in 1281 that he'd been assaulted at the church door in Northwold, then maimed and imprisoned by Benedict, the prior of Shouldham, along with Brother John de Shouldham and ten other named men. He said that afterwards they broke into his house at Stoke Ferry and stole away his goods. He repeated the complaint of trespass in 1294, although it's not clear what the original argument was between them or how it was eventually settled.

Football – and death

In 1321, there was a terrible accident at the priory during a game of football. Canon William de Spalding was playing football when his friend (also named William, but not a canon) collided with him and was wounded on a sheathed knife carried by Canon William. He died six days later; Canon William was extremely upset and blamed himself, but the pope decreed it was an accident and gave him a dispensation.

Fire, floods and gales

There were huge floods – involving both the sea and rivers – in 1392, and the priory was badly affected. Pope Boniface appropriated Caister Church to help them financially.

Scandals

Thomas Legh and John Ap Rice's scandalous comperta of 1536 claims that two of the nuns and three of the monks admitted 'incontinence' (in other words, they didn't keep their vow of celibacy), but the other visitations simply don't back up the claims.

Dissolution

The priory was dissolved in October 1538 and sold to Thomas Mildmay in 1553 for £1,049 9s 4½d (equivalent to just over a quarter of a million pounds in today's money).

According to Pevsner, the last of the walls were removed in 1831. During the ninteenth century, stained glass, several stone coffins and a skull in a vessel were found. Other stone coffins have been found there, along with Roman coins and a Roman road.

Thetford Castle

Thetford Castle is really two remains in one – an Iron Age fort, which was used as the bailey of an eleventh-century castle, and a chalk motte used for the castle itself. It's located just off Castle Street in Thetford (OS map reference TL 875 828) and is open to the public.

The Iron Age fortress

The earliest part of the castle site is formed by the double ramparts, which are thought to be earthworks of an Iron Age fortress dating back to between 100BC and 400BC. The fortress was built to control the fords which carry the Icknield Way across the Little Ouse and the River Thet.

What happened to the original inhabitants of the fortress isn't known, but it's thought that the earthworks may have been used as the

The castle motte, with the two enhanced Iron Age ramparts in the foreground.

winter base for the Danish army which occupied Thetford in 869 just before they defeated and killed the Edmund, the king of East Anglia (later St Edmund).

Battles against the Danes

A little further to the north is Wretham Heath, where Ulfcytel and his army made a stand against Sweyn Forkbeard in 1004, after he'd broken the truce he'd made with Ulfcytel and the councillors in East Anglia. Ulfcytel couldn't stop the Danes going back to their ships, but he and his troops fought heroically – as the Anglo-Saxon Chronicle points out:

> Swa hi sylfe sædon, þæt hi næfre wyrsan handplegan on Angelcynne ne gemitton þonne Ulfcytel him to brohte.

> (As they themselves said, that they never met with worse hand-play [i.e. combat] among the Englishmen than Ulfcytel brought to them.)

The castle motte, 25 metres high.

Ulfcytel won the Battle of Ringmere against Thorkell the Tall and the Danes in May 1010 (towards the south of the town), and was eventually killed at the Battle of Assandun in October 1016.

The beginning of the castle

Shortly after the Norman Conquest, the motte was raised in the middle of the earthworks and the defensive ditches were made taller (the ramparts are now 30 feet high). The motte is 80 feet high, measures 840 feet east to west, and is reputedly the second-tallest medieval earthwork in the country (next to Silbury). The base of the mound is almost 1,000 feet in circumference, but the top of the hill has a circumference of only eighty-one feet, with a dip (possibly a hiding pit) in the centre, so the castle couldn't have been particularly large.

The castle itself is thought to have been built shortly after the Norman Conquest, possibly by Ralph de Guader before his rebellion (see Norwich Castle, page 98) or more likely by Roger Bigod, Ralph's successor as Earl of Norfolk (who also built the Cluniac priory at Thetford – see page 125). At the time of the

121

Domesday survey, Thetford was the sixth largest town in the country; however, its importance declined after then, the wooden structure wasn't replaced by a stone keep.

The end of the castle

During the civil war between Stephen and Matilda, Hugh Bigod (son of Roger) supported Stephen. On rumours of Stephen's death in 1136 Hugh seized Norwich castle (see page 101). He was keen to extend his lands in Norfolk, and he rebelled twice against Stephen – and then in 1141 he defected to Matilda, who made him earl of Norfolk. When Hugh surrendered Ipswich Castle to Stephen in 1153, Stephen made him an earl and gave him the third penny from Norfolk.

Henry II, after his coronation, regranted the earldom of Norfolk to Hugh – but in 1157 he confiscated all the castles belonging to William de Blois and Hugh Bigod, including Thetford, and installed his own garrison at Thetford. The castle was eventually dismantled in 1173.

According to Samuel Lewis, writing in 1831, a 'perfect nautilus' was found in the vicinity of the castle and given to the British Museum.

In the 1870s, it was suggested that a waterworks could be built on top of the mound. Instead, the site was turned into a park and opened to the public in 1906, and Thetford Corporation bought the site for £25 in 1921.

Legends

There are several legends about the mound and exactly what's under it. One is that when the Cluniac priory (see page 125) was dissolved, six or seven silver bells from the priory were buried under the mound.

Another legend is that there was once a castle full of treasure on the site, and when the castle was being attacked the king ordered his men to build a mound over the whole lot. This may however be an ages-old confusion with the story of a different hill – because a treasure-hoard was actually found in a hill nearby. Gallow's Hill, to the north of the town, was an important Iceni religious site, and in 1979 the Thetford Treasure was found on the hill. This was a fourth-century hoard which included gold and silver braclets, jewellery with precious stones, and 33 silver spoons with inscriptions to Faunus, the woodland fertility god.

Yet another legend says that the devil made the castle mound; after he dragged his foot along the ground to create the Fossditch, he scraped the mud off his boot and the resulting clod of earth formed the castle hill. And if you walk round the hill seven times at midnight, it's said you'll get to meet him…

Remains of the church of the Holy Sepulchre at Thetford.

Thetford Church of the Holy Sepulchre

The church of the Holy Sepulchre is the remains of the twelfth-century church of the canons of the Holy Sepulchre, about 140 metres from the London Road (OS map reference TL 862 831).

Beginnings of the church of the Holy Sepulchre

There were only six houses of the canons of the Holy Sepulchre in England; they were set up to assist pilgrims visiting the shrine built on the site of Christ's burial chamber in Jerusalem. The remains of the church here is the only remains of the Holy Sepulchre canons in England. The canons of the Holy Sepulchre followed

123

the rule of St Augustine and were known as black canons; they were incorporated into the Augustinian order in the fourteenth century.

The monastery was founded between 1139 and 1145 by William de Warenne, the third Earl of Surrey, who was a crusader (see Castle Acre, page 32).

Scandals

Bishop Nix visited the house in June 1514 and discovered there were major problems. Thomas Vicar, the prior, accused Canon William Brigges of being an apostate (i.e. leaving the religious without permission – apparently at the time he'd gone to Snoring) and of living an 'evil life'. Canon Richard Skete complained about the awful beer – but then added that there was more of a problem with the prior's servant Stephen, who was supposedly in charge of the dairy. Stephen had married a woman of suspicious morals, he'd spent the profits from seven cows, and he'd 'laid violent hands' on Richard. He was backed up in his complaints by four of the other canons, who added that the buildings were in bad repair, the silver plate and spoons had been pawned, and the prior hadn't presented any accounts for seven years. Nix's judgements were not preserved, but it's likely that he ordered the prior to produce accounts with the help of someone elected from the priory.

Thomas Legh and John Ap Rice visited at the end of 1535 and claimed that Prior Clerk confessed he was 'incontinent' (in other words, he didn't keep his vow of celibacy) and wanted to get married; they also reported that three other canons were unchaste.

Dissolution

The house was originally set up for eight canons, but by 1520 the prior and two canons were all that were left. The priory was one of the poorest houses in East Anglia, worth only £40. It was suppressed in 1536; the site was granted to Sir Richard Fulmerston and the buildings were converted to a farm.

Spooks

In 1937, people heard singing in Latin in the ruins of the building, followed by the reading of a single text – the monks, perhaps? The chanting was heard again in the 1950s, one afternoon, and a local music teacher wrote down the tune. She spent a couple of years researching it, and eventually traced it back to the eleventh century… but nobody ever discovered who was singing or why.

Thetford Cluniac Priory

Remains of the Cluniac priory at Thetford.

Remains of the presbytery at Thetford Cluniac Priory.

The remains of Thetford Cluniac Priory and its fourteenth-century gatehouse lie just off the B1107 in Thetford (OS map reference TL 862 833). The priory is in the care of English Heritage and is open to the public.

The beginnings of the priory

The priory was founded by Roger Bigod for twelve Cluniac monks and was dedicated to the honour of St Mary.

Work began in July 1104, and the building work originally started next door to the church of St Mary the Great – which had been used as the diocese's cathedral church while the see was being removed to Norwich – on the Suffolk

Remains of the fourteenth-century gatehouse at Thetford Cluniac Priory.

side of the river. However, three years later, Malgod, the prior, was recalled to Lewes and replaced by Stephen. Stephen didn't like the site of the priory because he thought it would be too small, and he appealed to Roger Bigod and the king; he persuaded them to move the priory to a more open space on the Norfolk side of the river.

There was a huge row in 1107 when, only a week after laying the foundation stone, Roger Bigod died. He had asked to be buried in Thetford; however as the new church hadn't yet been built, the bishop seized Bigod's body and buried it in Norwich Cathedral instead. The monks protested to Henry I – but the king sided with the bishop, and the founder's body was never laid inside the priory.

The monks were finally able to move into the monastery on St Martin's Day (11 November), 1114.

Death at the priory, 1248

The first prior Stephen worked really hard for the good of his house – but the second prior Stephen was his complete opposite. Prior Stephen II was a monk of

Cluny, born in Savoy and claiming to be a relative of the queen. He was appointed before 1240, and invited his two brothers – a knight called Bernard and a clerk to Guiscard – to come to the house at Thetford. The monastic chronicler Matthew Paris describes the latter as a *'clericus monstruosis'*.

Stephen used to stay up all night with his brothers, eating and drinking and carousing until cock-crow. He didn't bother going to matins, mass or any other of the monastic services; he ignored the poor's requests for aid; and, if Bernard went away, Guiscard would eat all the monks' food before sneering at them and insulting them. (Matthew Paris describes the clerk's belly as being like a wagon laden with corpses in the frost – clearly making the point that the poor were dying with hunger while Guiscard was being a complete glutton.)

In 1248, the monk Stephen de Charun arrived at the priory from Cluny. Prior Stephen decided to send him back and started abusing him – which was a huge mistake, because Stephen de Charun was known for his hot temper. Aggravated by the prior's treatment of him, Stephen de Charun pulled out his dagger and stabbed him several times – and Prior Stephen died on the doorstep of the church. No doubt the monks were relieved that, with Prior Stephen gone, his horrible brothers would also leave... but they had to do the right thing and arrested the murderer, handing him over to the bishop.

The queen wanted vengeance for her kinsman and nagged the king continually until he ordered the bishop to hand Stephen de Charun over to him. He then ordered his men to put the monk in chains, put out his eyes and throw him into the deepest dungeon in Norwich Castle, where the monk eventually died.

Kidnapping and runaways, 1301

When Prior Vincent died in 1301, a row broke out over his successor. Thetford wanted to break away from Cluny and appoint one of their own monks, Reginald de Montargi, as the prior; but Cluny wanted to appoint someone else. The bishop of Norwich appointed Reginald, who resisted the abbot of Cluny. When the abbot sent some monks to sort it out, Reginald put them in prison and treated them badly, assuming that he was safe to do so because he had the protection of the bishop of Norwich and the Bigod family (i.e. the Earl of Norfolk).

Meanwhile, one of the monks at Thetford, Henry de Wangeford, escaped to the neighbouring house of Augustine canons. One of the canons, Richard de Harpele, and some of the servants gave him an armed escort towards Elveden – but Prior Reginald caught up with him. After a fight, Henry was taken back to the priory at Thetford and put in prison for two months, until he managed to escape again.

The abbot sent Thomas de Mountargys from Lewes to Norwich to talk to the bishop; but while Thomas was sitting reading in the cemetery of Norwich Priory Roger Bigod and his friends grabbed him, carried him out of the cemetery and put thirty men at the gates to stop him going back into Norwich Priory. Thomas sought refuge in the cemetery at St George's Tombland, opposite the cathedral, but two of the earl's men went over, beat him up and cut off part of his hood. A passer-by remonstrated with them, and Bigod's men responded by assaulting him. Afraid, Thomas fled to the church of the Friars of the Sack (which was roughly where St Andrew's Hall stands now). Bigod's men followed him, locked him in and kept him there until the next afternoon, so Thomas missed his appointment with the bishop.

Cluny was appalled at this treatment and complained to the pope. Boniface sent his commissioners to sort it out; he told them to release the imprisoned monks and warn Roger Bigod and his brother John to stop interfering. He added that if they disobeyed, they were all to be sent to him. Clearly the result was in favour of Cluny, because in 1302 Ralf de Frezenfeld was appointed prior of Thetford.

Riot and murder, 1313

In 1313, a mob broke into the priory. They assaulted Prior Martin de Rinhiaco and his servants; when they monks fled to the church for sanctuary, the mob followed them and murdered some of them in front of the high altar before carrying away goods from the priory. In August, a commission of *oyer* and *terminer* was appointed to look into the affair and give judgement. One man was accused of murdering the prior's nephew, but the jury found him not guilty; however, a year's protection was granted to Prior Martin.

Players to the king

But violence didn't characterise every single part of the priory's history. In 1498 Henry VII stayed at the Prior's Lodge, and the Waits from Norwich came to play for him; he paid them 1s 4d.

An extremely grand funeral

Thomas Howard, the seventh Duke of Norfolk, was buried in the choir of the priory church in June 1524. The funeral was incredibly grand; his body had lain in state at Framlingham for a month, and then travelled the 24 miles to the priory followed by over 900 mourners. At the priory, he was placed on a hearse covered with rich tapestries and banners, and according to David Dymond there were 700 lights as well. There were three masses, and then a knight, wearing the late duke's armour, was led on horseback down the nave. When the body was laid in the grave in front of the high altar, all the officers of his house broke their staves and threw them into the grave.

Allegedly the funeral cost £1,340 – the equivalent of almost £580,000 in terms of today's money – and that didn't include the massive stone tomb which covered the grave. The tomb was destroyed after the dissolution, and the duke's body was moved to Lambeth.

Dissolution

Thomas Legh and Richard Leyton visited in 1536 and stated that there were seventeen monks who confessed to very little. Thomas Wethirsett admitted to theft and Nicholas Horksley admitted to being 'unclean', but that was it. Legh and Leyton suspected a conspiracy of silence.

The Duke of Norfolk was unhappy at the idea of suppression because so many of his ancestors had been buried there (including his father, whose grand funeral is described above). He pointed out to the king that Henry's natural son, the Duke of Richmond, and his aunt (Lady Anne Howard) were buried in the priory, and he asked the king to convert the monastery into a secular church with a dean and chapter. Prior William would become the dean of the church and the monks would become secular canons; and in addition the Duke of Norfolk offered the king £1,000 (the equivalent of just over £400,000 in terms of today's money) and an annual pension of £100. The king agreed... but then changed his mind, and the abbey was dissolved in 1540. Just six weeks later, the Duke of Norfolk was granted the lands (for the sum of £1,000 and several manors in the south of England), and he moved the bones and tombs of several of his ancestors plus Henry's son to his family church in Framlingham, Suffolk.

The prior's lodgings was used a private house for the next 200 years, but was abandoned in 1737 when a tenant farmer removed its roof. The building had fallen into ruins by 1820.

Visions, relics and miracles

In the thirteenth century, a builder in Thetford was suffering from 'an incurable complaint' but had a dream that the Virgin Mary appeared to him and told him that he had to persuade the Prior of Thetford to build a Lady Chapel on the north of the church, and then he would regain his health. He had the dream three times, and when he told the prior, it impressed the prior enough to make him start building a wooden chapel.

The builder insisted that the chapel should be stone, rather than wood – he'd had a few more revelatory dreams. The Virgin Mary had also appeared to a woman in the town, and told her to go and chivvy the prior; when the woman didn't do as she was told, the Virgin Mary came back in another dream and touched her arm, and when the woman woke up she discovered that she'd lost the use of her arm. The woman was distraught and went to talk to one of the oldest monks at the priory, who advised her to offer an arm made of wax to the Holy Virgin. The woman did so, and the use of her arm was immediately restored.

Eventually the prior agreed to build a stone chapel, but he thought he'd save money on decorations by using a wooden image of the Virgin that had been brought from the old monastery but had been replaced long ago by a more beautiful one. The image looked a little scruffy, so the prior gave it to the monastery's painter to smarten it up. But when the painter removed the old paint, he saw a silver plate on the image's head. When the plate was removed, he discovered a hollow – and, inside the hollow were several precious relics, each wrapped in lead, with the name of each relic engraved on the lead wrappers. Either the relics were absolutely tiny or the hollow image was huge, because there was a huge list of relics, including:

A piece of Jesus' robe
A piece of the Virgin Mary's girdle
A piece of the rock of Calvary
A piece of the sepulchre from Jesus, the Virgin Mary and St John
A piece of Jesus' manger
Part of Lazarus' grave-clothes
Relics of various other saints – George, Agnes (a lock of hair), Barbara, Vincent, Leger, Gregory, Leonard, Jerome, Edmund (a piece of the coffin) and Etheldreda

There was also a letter from William at the church of Merlesham, addressed to Prior Stephen II, saying he'd sent them from Hugh Bigod at the church of the Holy Sepulchre in Jerusalem.

This amazing image and its contents were placed reverently in the new Lady Chapel, and then the priory saw some miraculous cures occurring. As a result, lots of pilgrims arrived, bearing offerings. With all this new money coming in, the new chapel more than paid for itself; it also meant that the church could be enlarged and five extra monks were added to the community.

Three particular miracles were written down in the fifteenth century. One was a woman who'd been struck dumb 'by a disease of her throat', and many people gave her money so she could make an offering to the image of the Virgin Mary; when she did so, the Virgin Mary came to her and pulled her tongue back up from her throat, and suddenly she was able to talk again. The second miracle was a resurrection case: a mother in Thetford had accidentally rolled on top of her child in the night and suffocated the baby. She laid it in front of the image, weeping and praying… and when she stopped praying, the baby was breathing again. The third miracle was the most incredible – again, a resurrection case. William Heddick, a carpenter, lived with his wife Isabel and their three-year-old son in the nearby village of Hockham.

One day, they were working in the field when their son fell asleep; the child was run over by a cart and they thought the child was dead – but the neighbours weren't so sure, and sent for the doctor. The doctor duly announced that he could see no signs of life. The Heddicks prepared for the funeral, and vowed to the Virgin Mary that if she would intercede and bring the child back to life, they would go on a pilgrimage to Thetford and make an offering to her statue. (There was a slight twist: they would take all their clothes off, first.) At midnight, the child revived – and the Heddicks did exactly as they'd promised, nudity and all!

Spooks

A monk has been seen at the priory, often on a summer afternoon, wearing a habit with the hood up to obscure his face. Whenever anyone goes to talk to him, thinking he's a practical joker or someone doing a living history event or guided walk, the monk simply vanishes into thin air.

The priory has also been featured on the 'Ghosthunters' documentary programme on the Discovery Channel, when parapsychologist C. J. Romer spoke about the beginnings of his career – back in 1984, he saw a figure dressed as a monk going down the stairs in the Prior's Lodge. He was with friends, and they ran over to the apparition – but as soon as they got there the stairs vanished...

Remains of the Prior's Lodge at Thetford, where the staircase and the monk mysteriously appeared and disappeared.

St George's Nunnery, Thetford

St George's Nunnery, Thetford, is the remains of a twelfth-century Benedictine nunnery. The remains are now incorporated into the headquarters of the British Trust for Ornithology, located just off Nun's Bridges Road in Thetford (OS map reference TL 872 822).

Nun's Bridges at Thetford, near the old nunnery.

The beginnings of the nunnery

The original religious house was said to be built by Uvius, the first abbot of Bury St Edmunds, some time before 1035; it was founded in memory of the soldiers who died nearby in around 870.

By 1160, the house was extremely poor and the two remaining canons, Toleard and Andrew, asked the abbot of Bury St Edmunds to let them withdraw. The abbot agreed, and decided to let the Benedictine nuns from Lyng (see page 81) come to the house in 1176.

Nun's Bridges take their name from the old nunnery (and they were once known as the Blue Bridges), but the crossing itself is very old – it's believed to be where the Icknield Way crossed the Little Ouse. The town's ducking stool was sited at the bridges during the middle ages.

Robberies, assaults and rotting food

After the nunnery's foundation, the monks of Bury St Edmunds sent them weekly supplies of food – one customary says that 96 gallons of beer and 35 loaves of bread were sent each week. Although the 12-mile journey seems short in modern terms, back then the roads weren't made up and the cooked meat in particular sent by Bury didn't travel well. The priory servants were often attacked and the good stolen, so in 1369 the abbot gave the nunnery an annual grant of 10 quarters of corn, 20 quarters of barley and 62 shillings (£3 2s, or the equivalent of about £940 in terms of today's money).

Scandals

The surviving visitation records show that for the most part the nuns led blameless lives. However, there is a notice from 1305 saying that the clerk William de Fornham and the chaplains Walter de Trofton and John Cat climbed over the priory wall one night and went to talk to the servant Joan de Fuldon. The nuns noticed a light shining under the door and went to investigate – and the men had to climb back over the priory wall very quickly! Rather horribly, in 1514 two of the nuns complained that the prioress was about to allow Dorothy Sturghs to become a novice – they objected because she was 'deaf and deformed'.

Dissolution

The nunnery was dissolved in February 1537. Elizabeth Hothe, the prioress, was given an annual pension of £5.

After dissolution, a mansion was built on the site and it eventually became a farm.

Spooks

Little George, Lord Dacre, is said to haunt Nun's Bridges. Some accounts of the story claim he was the ward of Sir Richard Fulmerston; others say that he'd been brought to the house by his stepfather Lord William Howard, son of the Duke of Norfolk, and was so happy there that Howard asked Fulmerston to let him stay. In May 1559, the seven-year-old was playing on his rocking horse when he fell off, cracked his head against the wall and shattered his skull. Allegedly, no matter how hard servants tried to shift the bloodstains, they remained there for 100 years. (The bloodstains that can't be scrubbed away feature in other Norfolk ghost stories, such as that linked with the Heydon family – see Baconsthorpe Castle, page 7.) Another version of the story says it was a vaulting horse rather than a rocking horse, and the pins at the feet were 'not made sure' so the horse fell on him and 'bruised the brains out of his head'.

After that, the ghost of the child rode around Nun's Bridges on a headless rocking horse. The blame was firmly pinned on Richard, with people saying that he'd deliberately made the horse unsafe so he could inherit his ward's property – even though Richard actually died three years before Lord Dacre did!

Apparently, the haunting was so bad that one day a group of local people threw a pound of new candles into the Little Ouse, telling the spirit not to come back until all the candles had burned. Another version of the story says that a clergyman had to lay the ghost. But there is an interesting parallel with his forebear Ranulph, Lord Dacre of Gilsland, who led Lancastrian forces at the battle of Towton in 1461. Ranulph was killed by an arrow when he removed his helmet to take a drink just as the Duke of Norfolk's forces arrived, and was buried in Saxton church in Yorkshire – upright, with his horse.

There's also a redbrick arch standing completely on its own nearby; it's the gateway to the nunnery precinct and dates from the sixteenth century. According to W. G. Clarke, writing in 1925, the gateway is blocked by a wall: it was built up seven times, and knocked down seven times, by a carriage with four horses.

The spa of Thetford

Between the castle and the site of the old nunnery, a chalybeate spring (i.e. the waters contained iron) was discovered in 1750. Nothing was really done about it until the water was analysed in the early nineteenth century and medical experts at the time thought that the water would be good for strengthening the digestive system and alimentary canal. So Thetford became a spa town; a gravel walk was laid out next to the river, called Spring Walk, and in 1818 Spring House was the pump room for the spa. However, the venture was unsuccessful and it was closed in 1839.

Thetford Warren Lodge

Thetford Warren Lodge.

Thetford Warren Lodge is a fifteenth-century warrener's lodge – there aren't many left in the country, so this one is significant and featured in David Dimbleby's TV series 'How We Made Britain'. It's located on the B1107 (the Brandon Road) about two miles west of Thetford (OS map reference TL 839 841). From the car park, go uphill on a sandy track between two old gateposts, and the ruins are a little way into the forest on the right. It's in the care of English Heritage and is open to the public.

The beginnings of the lodge

It's thought that the lodge was built around 1400 by the Prior of Thetford, to protect his gamekeepers and hunting parties against armed poachers. It's one of several lodges owned by the priory (others were at Norwick – on the border between Thetford and Croxton – Snarehill, Bodney and Santon) and is the best-preserved one. The walls are thick – up to a metre thick at ground level, and a drawing by Tom Martin in 1740 shows that it had a thatched roof as well as an octagonal watchtower.

The Normans had brought rabbits with them as a source of food and furs, and they were kept in enclosures by warreners who fed them and protected them from foxes and poachers before eventually harvesting them. Rabbit meat was expensive at first – up to five times the price of chicken – but became cheaper in the fifteenth century when the rabbits became more plentiful. It was still a luxury food, used at feasts; in 1465, when the Archbishop of York was installed, the menu included 4,000 rabbits.

When the warren at Thetford was set up, the area around the lodge wasn't wooded. In terms of economics, the landscape was perfect for warrens; the land wasn't very fertile, so crops were difficult to grow and rabbit warrens meant that the land would have an economic use. Physically, it suited the rabbits; the sandy Breckland soil was easy for them to burrow into, and the area has one of the lowest rainfalls in the country and warm summers, so it was similar to the Mediterranean climate the rabbits were used to.

It could take up to a year for rabbits to adapt to a new warren, so the warrener had to bore holes for burrows at first. He also had to feed the rabbits; in summer, there would be groundsel and dandelions, and in winter there would be turnips (Thetford warren had 80 acres of turnips for winter feed) and chopped-up furze.

Warreners tended to live in fortified houses so they could keep watch for poachers; Thetford Warren Lodge is typical in that it's two-storey. The warrener lived on the top floor of the lodge, and the ground floor was used for hanging the meat and drying and tanning the skins. There's a murder hole just above the doorway, so the warrener could drop rocks or unpleasant substances straight onto unwelcome visitors.

The fur produced at Thetford was silver-grey and very valuable. Although the Priory leased out its warrens, it was still able to give rabbits as gifts – David Dymond notes that in 1498/9, the priory presented Henry VII with 24 rabbots, and also gave Cardinal Wolsey 20 pairs of rabbits in 1520. The priory also bought rabbits from the warrens – they bought 824 rabbits at a cost of £3 3s in 1535/6 (equivalent to just over £1,200 in terms of today's money, or about £1.50 per rabbit).

After dissolution

After the dissolution of the monasteries, the warren was sold. However, it was one of the most productive rabbit warrens in the Brecks and the lodge was still used by warreners in the eighteenth century – when the defensive bank round the warren stretched for around eight miles – and in the nineteenth century the meat was sent to London (an incredible 30,000 carcasses a year) while the furs went to the two skin processing factories in Brandon. In the 1880, the Ground Game Act meant that farmers could kill rabbits on their own land, so the warreners no longer had a monopoly; there was also competition from French and Belgian imports, and developments in farming meant that the land could be used for crops. Gradually, the warrens fell out of use.

Marharajah Duleep Singh had a 99-year lease on the warren and planted trees there. Thetford Forest was planted in the 1920s and the rabbits became a nuisance – and rather horribly in the 1950s they were culled by the introduction of the disease mxyomatosis, which reduced their numbers by around 90 per cent.

The thatched roof of the warren lodge was destroyed by fire in 1935, as were the outbuildings that had been attached to it in the nineteenth century, and the lodge fell into ruin.

Spooks

Some tales say that the warren lodge was formerly a leper's house; however, there's some confusion here as a leper's graveyard has been found near Redcastle, which is nearer to Thetford (and only earthworks survive of the castle). Allegedly, one of the lepers still haunts the area: the gibbering figure has a (rather horribly) two-dimensional white face and burning eyes.

There's also a legend that a white rabbit with burning eyes haunts the area – very fitting for a former warren, but it'll bring disaster to you if you see it…

Another view of Thetford Warren Lodge.

Walsingham Priory

W alsingham Priory is the remains of an eleventh-century Augustinian priory, located off the High Street in Little Walsingham (OS map reference TF 934 368); it is open to the public. Walsingham Priory was the second most famous pilgrimage place in England (the most famous was Canterbury) and several monarchs are known to have been pilgrims. Apparently even Henry VIII, who eventually dissolved the priory, walked barefoot to Walsingham and offered a very expensive necklace to the Virgin Mary.

Arch – priory remains at Walsingham.

Sketch of excavations at Walsingham Priory from the 1820s, from Henry Harrod's Castles and Convents of Norfolk, 1856. *Photograph by author.*

A pilgrim's path, which went from Cambridge to Walsingham via Newmarket and Fakenham, was known as the Pilgrim's Way. It was also known as the Milky Way, as one of the relics at Walsingham was a vial of the Virgin's Milk.

The beginnings of the priory

The original chapel was built by Richelde (or Richeldis) of Faverches following her dream of 1061. Her son Geoffrey was in the First Crusade in 1095 and donated land to her for building an Augustinian priory. Work started in 1153, and it became famous as a place of pilgrimage. Henry III and Edward I both visited the priory; Henry gave 40 oaks to the church in 1232 and 20 for the guest house two years later.

Walsingham Priory ruins, plate from Thomas Kitson Cromwell's Excursions Through Norfolk, volume 2, 1819.

By the fifteenth century, Walsingham was the richest priory in Norfolk and Roger Ascham, when visiting Cologne in 1550, remarked: 'The Three Kings be not so rich, I believe, as was the Lady of Walsingham.' But the amount of wealth also brought corruption, and the bishops' visitations are full of scandalous behaviour.

The dream of Richeldis

In 1061, Richeldis prayed to the Virgin Mary to ask how she should honour her. In a dream, she was taken to Nazareth to see the *Sancta Casa* or House of the Annunciation, and Mary told Richeldis to build a replica at Walsingham. Richeldis decided to do exactly that, but there were two pieces of land, 200 paces apart, which seemed to fit the instructions Richeldis had been given. She chose one, but building didn't progress well; no matter how much they tried, the builders couldn't get the timbers to fit together. Richeldis prayed for guidance, and in the morning the building work had miraculously been transported to the other site – and it was also assembled much better than the builders could have done.

The story is told in the Walsingham Ballad, which was written around 1460 and printed by Richard Pynson in 1495 – it's sometimes known as the Pynson Ballad because of this. A version of part of the song is sung by Ophelia in Act IV of *Hamlet* as the first of her 'mad songs'.

Scandals, debts and 'evil living'

In March 1384, there was a row in the priory – John Snoryng, the prior, wanted to be abbot and had wasted the revenues of Walsingham in his attempts to secure the position. He was also accused of interfering with the weekly market, placing windows and doors in the priory wall on the market site. The chancellor, Michael de la Pole, headed the inquiry and placed the prior in the care of the sub-prior – but just over a week later John Snoryng was allowed to go back to being prior on condition he agreed to three recognizances of 1,000 marks (£666, 6 shillings and 8d each – equivalent to over a quarter of a million pounds each in terms of today's money) to pledge him to keep the priory without wasting the revenues until the next Parliament, and also he wasn't allowed to appeal to the pope regarding the matter. (If he didn't keep to the terms of the agreement, the recognizances meant that he had to pay the money.) He was eventually suspended three years later and removed from office because of further financial irregularities.

In 1494, when Bishop Goldwell carried out the visitation, things clearly weren't well – the record says the prior was afraid to say all he knew. But things grew much worse when William Lowth became prior in 1503. In 1514, Bishop Nix examined the prior and 31 canons and discovered that the prior led a scandalous life – at night, he went into the chapel and took his pick of the treasures that pilgrims had left, was brutal to the canons, and had warned them that anyone who told the bishop about him would suffer hugely for it. Lowth also kept a fool to amuse his friends and allowed him into Eucharist, didn't bother attending matins, and was having an affair with the wife of a servant. Several of the canons had followed his example – they left the bounds of the priory without leave, they spent much of their time in taverns, and argued all the time. Some of them had even broken into the cellar, stolen wine and spent all night drinking before going into the chapel and snoring through the services.

William was forced to resign – though, shockingly, he was allowed to become prior at West Acre (see page 144). Richard Vowell was appointed prior, and managed to get the priory back on track; at the final visitation of 1532, the bishop reported that '*omnia bene*'.

Famous pilgrims and their 'deliverances'

Edward I was a staunch supporter of Walsingham. On one occasion, he was playing chess with one of his knights; he left the table and a huge stone fell from the ceiling onto the spot where he'd been sitting. The king claimed that the miracle was due to Our Lady of Walsingham.

In 1314, according to an old manuscript reported by the eighteenth-century historian Francis Blomefield, Sir Raaf Boutetort was being chased by an enemy on horseback and was very close to being caught when he prayed to the Virgin Mary for deliverance. At the time he was heading towards a small wicket door at the entrance to the priory gates. Allegedly it was difficult for anyone to get through the door on foot, as it was 'not past an elne hye, and three quarters in bredth' (an ell was 45 inches – so that made this door a little under four feet tall and two and a half feet wide). However, Ralph prayed, and found himself the other side of the door in the sanctuary of the priory. The story was engraved onto a copper plate, along with a picture of the knight on horseback, and nailed to the priory door in remembrance.

The Pastons went to pilgrimage at Walsingham. When John Paston was ill in 1443, his wife Margaret wrote to him to say that her mother had promised an image of wax to the shrine – and it was a huge image, because it weighed as much as he did. Margaret had also pledged to go on a pilgrimage to the shrine for his sake.

Henry VI visted Walsingham in 1455; Edward IV went in 1469, and the Duke and Duchess of Norfolk travelled to Walsingham from Framlingham on foot in 1471.

Henry VII went to Walsingham at Easter 1487, when he was staying in Norwich. He prayed for help – and when he was victorious in battle at Stoke, shortly afterwards, he sent his banner as an offering to Walsingham. He also left them an image of silver-gilt in his will.

Arthur Plantagenet, the illegimate son of Edward IV and the admiral of the English fleet, was in a ship that ran into rocks off the French coast. He called out to Our Lady of Walsingham and said he would not eat fish or flesh until he visited her shrine if she would save the ship. The ship was saved, and Arthur kept his promise.

When Katharine of Aragon wrote to the king to tell him about the victory of Flodden in 1513, she said, 'and now go to Our Lady at Walsingham, that I promised soo long agoo to see'.

Preparing for Dissolution

In 1536, Sir Thomas Lestrange and Mr Hogges visited the priory at the request of Sir Richard Southwell; their duties were to sequestrate valuables such as money, plate and jewels. Southwell wrote to Cronwell claiming that there was an alchemist at Walsingham who might have been using a 'philosopher's stone' to 'multiply' money. It was probably just an ordinary laboratory, but the letter describes it in fascinating detail:

> Emoung other thinges the same Sir Thomas Lestrange and Mr. Hoges dyd there fynd a secrete privye place within the howse dyd ever come, as they saye, in wiche there were instrewmentes, pottes, bellowes, flyes of suche strange colors as the lick none of us had seene, with poyses and other thinges to sorte, and dewyd gould and silver, nothing there wantinge that should belonge to the arrte of multyplying. Off all wiche they desyred me by lettres to advertyse you, and also that from the

Satredaye at night till the Sonday next folowinge was offred at their now beinge xxxiijs. iiijd. over and besyd waxe. Of this moultiplying it maye please you to cawse them to be examyned, and so to advertyse unto them your further pleasure.

The Walsingham conspiracy

Henry VIII himself patronised Walsingham – in 1509 he paid his priest William Halys 100s (the equivalent of just over £2,500 in terms of today's money) for half a year's wages, for singing there, plus spent 46s 8d on burning the 'king's candle' there; in 1511 and 1512 he paid for glazing at the chapel; the king's candle was still burning in 1515, at a cost of 46s and 8d; and again in 1528, when he paid 43s 4d at Lady Day for the candle plus £5 for a mass (the equivalent of £810 for the candle and nearly £1,900 for the mass in terms of today's money). So it's unsurprising that the population wasn't happy at the idea of Walsingham being suppressed.

In 1537, the magistrates took depositions about a possible rising: George Gysburgh of Walsingham had suggested that the commons should rebel. He confessed to speaking with Ralph Rogerson about a potential rising against the suppression of the monasteries. The magistrates acted swiftly to find the rest of the conspirators: on information by Mr Watson, they seized Nicholas Mileham, the sub-prior of Walsingham. They wrote to Cromwell to say they thought Gysburgh, his son and Rogerson would confess more readily to him than to them.

Although the conspirators had done no more than talk about it, the rising was taken seriously. In May 1537 a special commission sat at Norwich Castle and sentenced eleven people to be executed for high treason – hung, drawn, beheaded and quartered. Just to make it clear their spies were everywhere, they held the executions in several different places. Ralph Rogerson and four others were executed at Norwich on 26 May; two days later, there were two more executions at Yarmouth; two days later, Nicholas Mileham and George Gysburgh were executed at Walsingham; and finally on 1 June George's son William and a Carmelite friar, John Pecock, were executed at King's Lynn. Several others were sentenced to life imprisonment.

Dissolution...

Thomas Legh and Richard Leyton visited the priory in 1536 and claimed in their comperta that six of the canons confessed to being incontinent (in other words, they didn't keep their vow of celibacy – which was more likely to be true under the rule of Prior Lowth than of Prior Vowell). They added that there seemed much superstition in 'feigned relics and miracles'.

The priory was dissolved in July 1538, and the priory site was granted to Thomas Sidney, master of the hospital for Little Walsingham. The prior – who'd bribed Cromwell with a 'poor remembrance' of £100 (the equivalent of over

£37,000 in terms of modern money – hardly 'poor'!), and who'd been commended as the person who'd taken 'one of the most rank traitors' in the conspiracy (i.e. Nicholas Mileham, the sub-prior) – was given a pension of £100. The statue of the Virgin Mary was taken to London to be burnt.

...and further disobedence

In 1564, the magistrate Sir Roger Townsend wrote to Cromwell; an old lady of Wells told a tale of a miracle done by the image of the Virgin Mary after it had gone to London. Sir Roger examined her, then put her in the stocks on a snowy January market day. He had her put in a cart with a paper on her head saying 'a reporter of false tales'; the cart carried her through the streets and lingered among the crowd, with 'young peoples and boyes of the town castyng snowballes at her'. Then she was put in the stocks until the market closed. The punishment was very harsh; but it was also very much a reflection of its time. As Townsend said to Cromwell:

> Thys was her penans; for I knewe no lawe otherwyse to punyshe her butt by discretion; trustyng itt shall be a warnyng to other lyght persons in such wyse to order their self. Howebeitt, I cannot perceyve but the seyd Image is not yett out of sum of ther heddes.

The wishing wells of Walsingham

There are two wells at Walsingham. The folklorist Enid Porter states that the wells were once thought to cure diseases of the head and stomach, then were credited with the power of granting any wish. There was a specific ritual to go through: you had to kneel on a stone between the wells, make a wish in silence, then drink as much water as you could hold in the hollows of your hands. Another version is that you had to be silent within ten feet of the water, kneel at each well in turn, make a wish and keep it secret, and it would come true.

The Walsingham Way

The eighteenth-century historian Francis Blomefield reported that it used to be believed that the Milky Way pointed to the residence of the Virgin Mary – so in Norfolk, the Milky Way was actually called the Walsingham Way.

Tunnels

As with many religious houses, there is a story of a secret tunnel. The one at Walsingham is meant to connect it with the priory at Binham – however, the tale of the tunnel is much more interesting at the Binham end (see page 13).

West Acre Priory

The fourteenth-century gatehouse of West Acre Priory is the remains of the eleventh-century Cluniac priory at West Acre, next to the church on Low Road (OS map reference TF 780 150).

Beginnings of the monastery

The Augustinian priory at West Acre was founded by Ralph de Toni, the standard-bearer of Normandy, in around 1100; it was dedicated to All Saints and

St Mary. Ralph's sons Oliver and Walter entered the monastery.

Disaster

There was a huge fire in 1286 on the Nativity of St Mary (8 September); according to the chroniclers John of Oxenedes and Florence of Worcester, the priory, church and the conventual buildings were all destroyed.

Remains of the gatehouse of the priory at West Acre.

Scandals

At Bishop Goldwell's visitation in 1494, he discovered that the prior, Richard Palle, was elderly and had lost control of the priory. Whenever Palle gave commands, they were ignored or the subprior, Edmund Lichfield, contradicted him. Several of the monks were lazy and stirred up trouble. Lichfield was insolent and spent his time farming a rabbit warren and rearing swans – and gave the rabbits and swans to gentlemen as presents, so they cost the priory money instead of making money. There is no record of Goldwell's instructions, but four years later Lichfield became prior in a different religious house.

In 1514, the priory was in financial trouble. Richard Clarke, the prior, said he was in debt for £20 (equivalent to nearly £9,000 in terms of today's money) and couldn't pay the stipends of the canons; their sheep stock had diminished hugely, and they had no grain apart from the amount they'd bought. There was also much

West Acre Priory gatehouse, plate from Thomas Kitson Cromwell's Excursions
Through Norfolk, *volume 2, 1819.*

bickering among the canons, complaints against the subprior, and comments that
the prior relied too heavily on his servant John Smyth – which meant that people
outside the monastery could get influence with him through Smyth and Smyth's
wife. Canon Robert Pepyr was also upset because he was never granted leave of
absence – he was the only canon who could play the organ, and they needed him

to help with the services. Bishop Nix made them chose a new sub-prior, John Spilman, and William Smyth was dismissed.

Six years later, the house was even more in debt. William Lowth was the prior – the one who'd behaved so badly at Walsingham (see page 140). Although three of the canons called him a 'sensual person', the Victorian scholar Augustus Jessopp thinks that it probably means that Lowth was touchy and easily irritated; surprisingly, after the problems at Walsingham, there was no scandal attached to Lowth's name at West Acre.

Debts had increased again in 1526, despite the fact there was a different prior, William Wingfield. One canon, however, had a major scandal reported; details are incredibly sketchy and we don't know what the bishop's injuctions were.

After that, Prior Wingfield took over. At the visitation of 1532, all debts had been paid; however, Wingfield's sister had married into the Calibut family, who seemed to be getting preferment when they shouldn't have done so. Francis Calibut was known as an 'immoral' man but was still appointed pincerna to the priory (i.e. was responsible for their provisions). Several canons had deserted the priory, less bread had been given to the poor and the lamp hadn't been kept burning before the Sacrament.

Dissolution

According to thomas Legh and John Ap Rice, in 1535 the prior and eleven canons confessed to 'most flagrant acts of incontinency' (in other words, they didn't keep their vow of celibacy). It probably wasn't true – certainly not of Wingfield, or the king wouldn't have appointed him as a justice in the county or given him a pension of £40 a year.

The priory was dissolved in January 1538. The monks had a finger of St Andrew set in silver as its major relic; they said it was worth £400 (the equivalent of nearly £165,000 in terms of today's money) but they'd been forced to pawn it for £40. However, the commissioners at the Dissolution refused to redeem it, as they said it wasn't worth even a tenth of the pawned value!

The mystery of the headless and footless skeleton

According to the Reverend J. H. Bloom, in 1836, workers were clearing away soil at West Acre when they discovered a sarcophagus, upside down, placed over a shallow grave lined with cement. The grave contained a body wrapped in a shroud of sackcloth. Oddly, the head and feet had been removed before burial (at a neck vertebra and the ankle joints respectively), even though the sarcophagus was more than large enough to accommodate it and had the usual recess for a head. The medical man who examined the skeleton said the body was female, but nobody had any idea who she was or why her head and feet had been removed.

Weybourne Priory

Weybourne Priory is the remains of a thirteenth-century Augustinian priory, dedicated to the Blessed Virgin and All Saints. It lies next to the church on The Street (aka the A149) in Weybourne (OS map reference TG 112 433).

The beginnings of the priory

The priory was founded in around 1200 by Sir Ralph Mainwaring or Meyngarin) and was a cell to the priory of West Acre. It was built on the site of the existing Saxon church; most priory churches were built separately from the parish churches, or were built as large cruciform churches with the east part under the control of the monks and the west part under the control of the parish (as at Binham and Wymondham). In this case, they kept the old church's west tower, rebuilt the parish church to the south-west and built the monks' choir on the rest.

Remains of the priory at Weybourne.

Schisms, 1314

When Prior Roger de Hoxne died in 1314, there was a row; Weybourne wanted to choose their own prior (Henry, the sub-prior) but the prior of West Acre said that because they were a cell of his house they had to choose a canon from West Acre as their next prior.

It went to arbitration; Weybourne was granted the right to choose their own prior in future, but they also had to pay a pension to West Acre every year.

Clearly the house was small, because when Prior Elyngham died in 1422 there were only two canons left. The bishop said that there weren't enough canons to hold an election, so he co-opted John de Laxfield (one of the two canons) as the prior.

Visitations

The house remained poor; although at the 1494 visitation the conduct of the monks was good, Prior Clement hadn't been able to afford to pay one of his three canons. At the visitation of 1514, there was only one canon besides the prior, because they couldn't afford to keep even three canons there, let alone the seven they were originally meant to have.

Remains of the priory at Weybourne.

Dissolution

There was the usual assertion by the commissioners that the two monks in the house were 'of slanderous name' – though it's highly unlikely. The priory was dissolved in 1536 and its goods and chattels were sold to Thomas Pygeon in 1537 for 66s and 8d (the equivalent of around £1,359 in terms of today's money); there wasn't much, just six swine, a copper-gilt cross, a silver crucifix, a printed missal, a 'litill printed masse boke' and a few bits of furniture. The lands were granted to John Gresham, son of a London mercer.

Spooks, smugglers, and Black Shuck

The ghost at Weybourne isn't connected to the priory – he's the ghost who whistles on nights with a full moon, and has been identified with smuggler John Smythe.

John the smuggler had come to Weybourne with his crewmates for provisions. He stayed a while at the inn to flirt with the landlord's daughter; meanwhile, the Revenue men had learned that the smugglers were in the village and headed to the beach to try and trap them before they could go back to their ship. The other smugglers were tipped off and hurried back to the beach; they waited in their rowing boat for John, but when he didn't turn up they assumed the Revenue men had already caught him and they rowed back to their ship.

John arrived ten minutes later, saw them rowing out to sea, and whistled to them to attract their attention – but the Revenue men thought the whistle was a signal and came out of their hiding places. The sea was coming in and John couldn't swim – but he didn't want to take his chances with the Revenue men. He kept walking out towards the ship, whistling in the hope that his fellow smugglers would hear him and come to his rescue.

But then he lost his footing, sank beneath the waves and drowned.

So on moonlit nights in Weybourne, you can still hear him whistling to his fellow smugglers.

Smuggling definitely took place at Weybourne – the deep inshore waters are easy to navigate at Weybourne Hope, between the cliffs and the shingle spit of Blakeney point. There's even a saying that 'He who would all England win, should at Weybourne Hope begin', because ships could unload troops safely in the deep waters. (It was used to send troops off to France in the First World War.) Apparently the smugglers used to bury themselves in shallow pits in the shingle, up to their neck, until the ship carrying the contraband came into view. The local lord of the manor turned a blind eye, and the smugglers used to leave him parcels and barrels.

The smugglers also used the tale of Black Shuck to make people avoid the coastal path, particularly between Weybourne and Overstrand – nobody wanted to meet the huge black dog on a dark night. There are several different stories about Black Shuck. It's thought that his name derives from the Anglo-Saxon word *scucca*, meaning 'demon' – and he's apparently terrorised the East Anglian coast for the last thousand years. Black Shuck is meant to be the size of a small calf, with blazing eyes; and if you see him, you (or a member of your family) will go mad or die within the next year. Other suggestions are that Shuck is a folk memory from down the years – the Danes used to bring large black dogs with them on their ships, so he's associated with the raids and death. Some stories have him as a headless dog with one blazing eye, and it's thought that the smugglers used this by putting a black cloth over a small pony, hanging a lantern round its neck and sending it ahead of their contraband: nobody walking on a road meant to be haunted by the dog (i.e. the smuggling run) would wait about to see what the dark creature with a single blazing eye really was!

Another story is that Shuck the ghost of a huge black dog that was apparently found next to his master after a shipwreck at Salthouse in the early 1700s, and haunts that section of the coast on stormy nights, still howling for his master.

Arthur Conan Doyle heard the stories about Black Shuck while staying just down the coast at Happisburgh, and it inspired his story 'The Hound of the Baskervilles'.

Wymondham Abbey

The remains of the twelfth-century Benedictine abbey at Wymondham are at the side of the parish church in Church Street, Wymondham (OS map reference TG 106 013).

The beginnings of the abbey

The abbey was originally a priory, and was a cell of the Benedictine monastery of St Albans. It was founded in 1107 by William d'Albini, Henry I's chief butler, for a prior and twelve monks, and was dedicated to St Mary and St Alban. He gave it much land as well as tithes and rents, and also had permission from the king to move the road so it went by his house rather than by the church, where it had disturbed the monks.

Clashes between town and gown, 1249

William d'Albini wanted the townsfolk to be able to use the church, but didn't give any instructions as to who ruled over which part of the church. The prior wanted to rule over the whole building – and the townsfolk naturally resisted. There was a huge row in 1249, and Pope Innocent IV had to intervene. He ruled that the townsfolk would have the nave, north aisle and north-west tower (away from the monastic buildings) and the

The monks' tower at Wymondham Abbey.

monks would have the quire, the eastern chapels, the transepts, the south aisle and the central tower.

However, this led to more rows. The lantern tower was crumbling, so in the late fourteenth century the monks moved the bells to the parishioners' tower, demolished the old Norman tower and built a new octagonal one in 1376, finishing it in 1409. They put a solid wall across, took their bells back and rehung them in the new tower... and then walled up the entrance to the parishioners' tower.

The parishioners were furious – especially as Prior Walsingham then appropriated the vicar's income and claimed the right to appoint the townsfolk's priest. The bishop wasn't helpful, and there was a riot which ended with the prior seeking protection and 24 of the townsfolk bound over to keep the peace in July 1409. Having to pay large amounts of

Wymondham Abbey, viewed through ruined arch of the abbey.

money made them even angrier, and on St Bartholomew's Day (24 August) violence erupted again, with the monks being beaten by clubs and threatened with daggers.

In October 1409, the townsfolk hung three bells of their own in the north porch – and also filled in the two doors in the new wall behind their altar so the monks couldn't go into the nave. It got worse: a mob invaded the church and threatened the prior, who fled to his chamber – and Mass wasn't swung for Epiphany. The monks had to send for help, and the violence ceased when two of Sir Thomas Erpingham's men arrived to keep the peace.

The monks retaliated by indicting the townsfolk for hanging the bells and stopping up the wall. According to the monks, the church was theirs, and the townsmen should come at the sound of the abbey bells and none other.

Henry IV ordered the Archbishop of Canterbury to look into the dispute. The archbishop's judgement was that the townsfolk could keep their bells, but they mustn't ring them at times that would annoy the priory – in other words, between 6pm and 6am when the monks were resting. They were only allowed to ring the bells for divine service or for the dead, but there were some exceptions: Christmas day, Easter day and if the king, archbishop or bishop visited. They were also allowed to use the bell as a warning signal in case of 'any public enemies', thieves, robbery and fires.

The townsfolk still weren't happy, and 3,000 inhabitants signed a petition saying that their tower was so low, they couldn't hear their own bells. They asked the king if they could build a new, higher tower; and in the middle of the fifteenth century Sir John Clifton paid for the building of the new tower, 168 feet high, as well as the top of the nave. The building work took 66 years.

Becoming an abbey

As well as clashing with the town, the monks at Wymondham also clashed with the abbot of St Albans. In 1160, the abbot of St Albans ignored the William d'Albini's founding charter and said that he had the right to choose the prior and visit the priory whenever he wanted; the d'Albini family protested the charter said they could choose the prior. The row went on for years, with the abbot pushing his rights further and further. It got worse when Hugh became abbot of St Albans in the early fourteenth century – he was incredibly extravagant and burdened the priory with his whims, including giving Edmund, the infant son of Sir Simon de Hethersete a pension of 40s a year (the equivalent of over £650 in terms of today's money), payable by the priory of Wymondham. (Edmund lived until he was 50, so it cost the priory a small fortune.)

It came to a head in 1446 after Stephen London was made prior. Stephen had been the archdeacon at St Albans and the abbot loathed him – probably because Stephen spoke his mind and pointed out the abbot's faults. In order to get Stephen out of St Albans, the abbot made Prior Waleys resign, on the grounds that he was too old, and made Stephen the prior of Wymondham. A year later, the abbot visited, and was horrified to discover that Stephen was actually doing rather well and everyone at Wymondham liked him – including the patron of the priory, Sir Andrew Ogard.

The abbot ordered Stephen to resign, but Stephen refused; instead, together with Sir Andrew, he petitioned the king to let Wymondham become an abbey. For two hundred years, the abbots of St Albans had acted on a whim regarding Wymondham, and ignored the founders' charters. The original charter gave the founders' successors the right to turn the priory into an abbey, so the king agreed – and in 1448 they had a papal bull confirming that Wymondham could be an independent abbey. Stephen was the first abbot – and took great delight in sending a letter full of insults to the abbot of St Albans!

Scandals

The bishop's visitations uncovered some real scandals at Wymondham. In 1492, Bishop Goldwell had to listen to a huge stream of complaints all based around the inability of John Kyrteling, the abbot, to keep discipline: the divine offices were miserable and celebrated 'grudgingly', the monks weren't in cloister when they were supposed to be, and they mixed with lay people in the south of the church after prime.

The complain went on that some of the monks bought and sold goods as if they were merchants rather than religious people, and also went out hunting with dogs and hawks, which they weren't supposed to do. Others went out without the permission of the abbot, and some of the monks were too lazy to study their letters; they also weren't sticking strictly to the rule and ate more red meat than they were supposed to. The buildings, too were a mess: the precinct walls were badly repaired, as were the dorter and farmery, and the frater (refectory) was not guarded properly. Bishop Goldwell made Kyrteling resign in favour of John Redmayn.

Thomas Chamberlain was the next abbot, and when Bishop Nix did the visitation of 1514 things were even worse – despite the fact that only two of the monks from the 1494 visitiation were still alive. Chamberlain stated that the monks had broken the cloister bolts, and that the prior and other monks had broken open the evidence chest. William Bury, the prior, had a list of complaints – some were quite serious, such as Richard Cambridge attacking the doctrine of the resurrection, whereas others were very trivial, such as John Cambridge hiding a cookery book in his cubicle.

The monks in turn complained about the prior – and Thomas Lynn blew the whistle on Bury's behaviour. Bury was quite possibly insane, and was certainly charged with being a madman; his behaviour was violent and ill-tempered. Lynn testified that Bury drew a sword on Richard Cambridge, threw stones at Cambridge and John Harleston, threatened to kill John Wormell with a sword, smashed John Hengham's claricord on purpose, and only went to matins once a month. (However, Richard Cambridge also came in for some complaints: particularly being drunk, consorting with the wife of Mr Porter, and was given the nicknames of 'Dudley' and 'poller' – Edmund Dudley was a notorious extortionist in the reign of Henry VII, and a poller was a tax collector, so Cambridge clearly took money from people.)

Complaints about other monks included bad language, drunkenness, fights in the cloister and insolent servants. A big problem was that the monks went in and out of the abbey however they liked... and scandalous women came into the house. The chamberlain, James Blome, seemed to be particularly fond of the company of women – he was visited by the wife of Edward Colyns (the cook) and the wife of Mr Johnson, and also by 'the daughters of a certain widow residing in Le Dearie' (apparently the local bawdy house). John Hingham's chamber was visited by 'the wife of Angelus'. Some of the buildings were in ruins, and the church vessels and ornaments were in a mess.

The only injunction to survive was that the bishop dismissed the prior and told them to elect another. They removed him – but at the visitation of 1520 he was precentor, and in 1526 he was prior again.

At the 1520 visitation, although the new abbot John Holt had improved matters, there were more complaints of drunkenness and of monks not bothering to turn up to matins. The windows needed reglazing (it was noted that pigeons flew through them and defiled the choir books!), and the abbot wasn't rendering any accounts. This time, Nix gave more injunctions. The monks had to keep matins and were not allowed to drink after compline. They had to glaze the windows and restore the books and vestments; the abbot had to render his accounts properly, and there needed to be more food of better quality.

After Holt died, his successor William Castleton improved things still further. At the 1516 visitation, there was a complain that Thomas Osmund was a 'quarrelsome person', the monks didn't to the dormitory together after compline as they were supposed to do, and an instructor was needed for the four new notives. The bishop told them they had to appoint an instructor, repair the choir books and go to the dormitory together in future.

Spooks

Surprisingly, there are no tales of Wymondham Abbey being haunted. However, there have been some rather spooky discoveries at the abbey. On Christmas Eve 1833, while the churchyard was being enlarged, two lead coffins were found. In the coffins were a woman and prematurely born child, both embalmed. It's known that the founder, William d'Albini, and his wife Maud were buried before the high altar, and also that Maud died in childbirth, so archaeologists of the time believed that they'd discovered Maud and her baby.

Shortly after, two stone coffins were found at the entrance of the chapter house in the east cloister; they contained the remains of two monks, and each had been covered with coarse woollen cloth.

Interestingly, a lead ingot weighing a ton was also found; it had a royal stamp on it and had apparently lain in the chapter house since the dissolution.

Tunnels

As with so many of the religious houses, Wymondham Abbey has a legendary secret tunnel. This one was meant to connect the priory with the Green Dragon (a fourteenth-century pub which still remains on Church Street, and originally was next to the abbey gates). Allegedly, the tunnel was used by the monks when they misbehaved... but rather more prosaically, it was actually a drainage culvert.

Dissolution – and another riot

As usual, Thomas Legh and John Ap Rice visited the abbey, and claimed that four of the monks admitted that they were unclean (in other words, they didn't keep their vow of celibacy). The abbey was suppressed in 1538. The king retained ownership of the abbey for the next ten years, and his agent was the Hethersett lawyer John Flowerdew. Despite the fact that the townsfolk had bought certain parts of the church from the king, Flowerdew stripped it of lead and some of the stone, leaving the nave of the parish church open to the elements. He also ignored the contract between the king and the townsfolk and made it very difficult for them to buy back the bells and the lead.

One of the townsfolk instrumental in raising the money to pay the king was Robert Kett, who had also been responsible for looking after the church vessels and candles. He never forgave Flowerdew for his behaviour – so in 1549, when Flowerdew paid men to rip down fences around Kett's enclosures, Kett went one

*The Green Dragon in Church Street,
Wymondham: this was next to the original gate to
the abbey.*

better. He ripped the fences down himself, joined the rebels, and led them to Flowerdew's fences: no doubt he had great satisfaction in pulling them down.

The summer of 1549 had seen rising taxation and un-employment, plus droughts, food shortages and a huge rise in the population. When the local gentry started fencing off common lands, the poorer people had had enough and rebelled. Kett led the Norfolk rebels, and helped them draw up a list of 29 requests – including asking the king to stop enclosure and rack renting, to standardise meas-urements, to make rich priests teach the children of the poor and finally asked that 'all bond men may be made free, for God made all free with his precious blood shedding'.

Kett and his 20,000 rebels captured Norwich and gar-risoned it (though notably they neither sacked nor destroyed the city), but eventually the rebels were beaten by the Earl of Warwick's army. The rebel leaders were hanged, drawn and quartered; William Kett, Robert's brother, was hanged from the tower at Wymondham Abbey, while Robert was hanged in chains from Norwich Castle (see page 102). Robert was finally buried in an unmarked grave the following summer.

Although the city originally gave thanks for their delivery from the rebels, and even 100 years later there was a festival to celebrate Kett's defeat, the county's view of Kett has changed over the years. In 1949 commemorative plaque was put on the castle walls 'in reparation and honour to a notable and courageous leader in the long struggle of the common people of England to escape from a servile life into the freedom of just conditions.'

Appendix

Timeline from 1020 to the Restoration of the Monarchy 1660

Date	Events in the Norfolk castles and monasteries	Events in England
1020	St Benet's Abbey taken under Cnut's protection (though may have been an establishment on the site before 870)	
1061	Walsingham Priory founded	
1066		Norman Conquest
1067	Norwich Castle motte and bailey strengthened	
1067?	Thetford Castle motte raised (in middle of Iron Age earthworks)	
1070	Castle Acre Castle – building started in the 1070s	
1075	Siege at Norwich Castle	
1085		Domesday Book
1087		William the Conqueror dies; William Rufus crowned
1090	Castle Acre Priory founded	
1091	Binham Priory founded	
1096	Norwich Cathedral and Priory – building started	
1100	Norwich Castle – stone keep built; West Acre Priory founded	
1104	Thetford Cluniac Priory founded	
1105	Horsham Priory founded	
1107	Wymondham Abbey founded (as a priory – abbey status granted 1448)	
1133	Bromholm Priory founded	
1135	Blackborough Priory founded; Pentney Priory founded	Stephen crowned; civil war 1135-1148

Date	Events in the Norfolk castles and monasteries	Events in England
1138	Castle Rising Castle – building started	
1139	Thetford Church of the Holy Sepulchre founded	
1145	New Buckenham Castle – building started	
1146	Carrow Priory founded; Old Buckenham Priory founded	
1154		Henry II crowned
1170		Thomas Becket murdered
1173	Thetford castle dismantled	Baronial rebellion
1176	Lyng nunnery moved to Thetford (to site of house founded in 1030)	
1181	Crabhouse nunnery – land granted (the original nunnery was founded in the previous century)	
1185	Hickling Priory founded	
1189		Richard I crowned
1190	Shouldham Priory founded	Richard's crusade
1195	Langley Abbey founded	
1200	Hempton Priory founded (was originally a hospital 1135); Weybourne Priory founded	
1206	Creake Abbey founded	
1212	Siege at Binham Priory	
1215	Coxford Priory founded	John I signed Magna Carta
1216	Beeston Priory founded	
1249	Marham Abbey founded	
1256	Norwich Whitefriars founded	
1258-67		Revolt of the Barons
1263	Siege of New Buckenham castle	
1264	Greyfriars founded at King's Lynn	
1272	Siege at Norwich Cathedral Priory	
1283	Siege at Castle Acre Priory	
1287	Major storm surge on the East Coast – affected Hickling Priory and St Benet's Abbey	
1298		Model Parliament set up

Date	Events in the Norfolk castles and monasteries	Events in England
1307	Siege at Horsham Priory	
1312	Siege at Castle Rising Castle	
1319	Gresham Castle granted licence to crenellate	
1326-7		Isabella and Mortimer depose Edward II; Edward III crowned
1331	Isabella at Castle Rising Castle until 1358	
1338-1453		Hundred Years' War with France
1360	Ingham Priory founded	
1348-9	Plague at Hickling Priory	Black death killed a third of the population
1397	Castle Acre Castle derelict	
1381	Court rolls burnt at Binham Priory, Carrow Priory and St Benet's Abbey	Rising (aka Peasants' Revolt) and social upheaval
1388	North Elmham chapel fortified (built on 12th-century chapel)	
1400	Thetford Warren Lodge – building started	
1432	Caister Castle – building started	
1439	Plague at Hickling Priory	
1443	Siege (of sorts!) at Norwich Cathedral Priory	
1448/9	Siege at Gresham Castle	
1450	Baconsthorpe Castle – building started	
1451	Gresham Castle derelict	
1455-85		Wars of the Roses
1461	Siege of New Buckenham castle	
1469	Siege at Caister Castle	
1506	Creake Abbey dissolved after plague killed all the canons	
1509		Henry VIII crowned king
1529		Henry VIII head of the Church of England

Date	Events in the Norfolk castles and monasteries	Events in England
1536-40	1536: Coxford Priory, Hempton Priory (August), Hickling Priory, Horsham Priory, Ingham Priory, Langley Abbey, Marham Abbey, Old Buckenham Priory (September), Thetford Church of the Holy Sepulchre, Weybourne Priory 1537: St George's Nunnery, Thetford (February), Blackborough Priory (March), Bromholm Priory (February), Castle Acre Priory (November), Crabhouse Nunnery (January), Pentney Priory (February) 1538: Carrow Priory, Greyfriars (King's Lynn), Norwich Cathedral Priory (May), Norwich Whitefriars (November), Shouldham Priory (October), Walsingham Priory (July), West Acre Priory (January); Wymondham Abbey 1539: Beeston Priory (June), Binham Priory (May) 1540: Thetford Cluniac Priory	Dissolution of monasteries
1549	Kett's Rebellion	
1559		Elizabeth crowned queen
1588	Castle Rising Castle derelict	Spanish armada
1642-52		English Civil War
1649	New Buckenham Castle demolished	Commonwealth set up
1660		Restoration of the Monarchy

Selected bibliography

Martim de Albuquerque (ed), *Notes and Queries*, 1857

Francis Blomefield, *An Essay Towards A Topographical History of the County of Norfolk*, 11 volumes, London 1807

John Chambers (ed), *A General History of the County of Norfolk*, 1829

Thomas Kitson Cromwell, *Excursions Through Norfolk*, 2 volumes, London 1818-9

William Dugdale, *Monasticon Anglicanum*, 1817

W. A. Dutt, *The Norfolk Broads* (2nd editon), 1905

John Glyde, *Norfolk Garland*, Jarrold 1872

Henry Harrod, *Gleanings among the Castles and Convents of Norfolk*, Norwich 1857

M. R. James, *Suffolk and Norfolk – A perambulation of the two counties with notices of their history and their ancient buildings*, JM Dent, London 1930

Augustus Jessopp, *Visitations of the Diocese of Norwich*, Camden Society (vol 43), 1888

Richard Le Strange, *Monasteries of Norfolk*, Yates Publications 1973 [no ISBN]

Susan Swain Madders, *Rambles in an Old City*, London 1853

Frank Meeres, *Not of this world: Norfolk's monastic houses*, Blackall Books 2001, ISBN 0954115309

Claude J. W. Messent, *The Monastic Remains of Norfolk & Suffolk*, H.W. Hunt (14 Orford Hill, Norwich) 1934 [no ISBN]

W. Page (ed), *A History of the County of Norfolk Volume 2*, Victoria County History 1906

Nikolaus Pevsner and Bill Wilson, *The Buildings of England, Norfolk 1: Norwich and North-east* (2nd edition), Penguin 1997, ISBN 0140710582

Nikolaus Pevsner and Bill Wilson, *The Buildings of England, Norfolk 2: North-west and South* (2nd edition), Yale 2002, ISBN 0300096577

Enid Porter, *The Folklore of East Anglia*, B. T. Batsford Ltd, London 1974, ISBN 0713427930

Charles Sampson, *Ghosts of the Broads*, London 1931

Ernest R. Suffling, History and Legends of the Broad District, London 1891